# MOVE OVER, VIOLA

## CHRISTOPHER DAINTON

Copyright 2023 by Christopher Dainton

All rights reserved. No portion of this book may be reproduced, stored in a retrieval system, or transmitted in any form or by any means without the express written permission of the publisher. The only exception is by a reviewer, who may quote short excerpts in a published review.

*Move Over, Viola* endeavours to be as true as possible to the author's real-life experience. For privacy reasons, some names, locations, and dates may have been changed.

2023 Saturnine Trade Paperback Edition
www.saturninebooks.com

Published in Canada by Saturnine Books, Toronto.
ISBN: 9798591521738
Printed and bound in the United States of America
Book design by Nuno Moreira, NM DESIGN
Second edition, 2023

# MOVE OVER, VIOLA

A RACIAL JUSTICE MEMOIR

# CHRISTOPHER DAINTON

For my mother, whose story is better than most.

And for Avani, who tolerated my daily provocations.

# FOREWORD

*Move Over Viola* is fanciful hybrid of memoir and fiction, a plot pulled from dusty folders, old journals, essays, and envelopes strewn across a basement. It is about the ironies and contradictions of modern social justice, as demonstrated by the moribund legal case of my mother versus Bell Canada in the 1980s. The format was inspired by Kurt Vonnegut's *Cat's Cradle*, which consists of an archipelago of almost a hundred tiny chapters, a mosaic of tiny chips that's perfect for short attention spans. These seventy-three chapterettes came together by accident, as the narrative devoured court transcripts, newspaper articles, and correspondence, culminating in a true story that amplifies the real and historical for dramatic purposes.

This tale has two distinct perspectives whose relative merit is left to your judgment. It's not for those bothered by words like *mulatto* or *Negro*. I prioritized honesty over sensitivity and decided that if anyone can be blasphemous and incisive, it's one's son. That makes this a quixotic personal journey as much as a memoir. It's important that my mother read this while she's alive, so she can decide whether it does her story the justice that was denied to her.

# PART ONE

MOVE OVER, VIOLA

# 1. SIMULACRA AND SIMULATION

I thought getting my mother's Negro face onto the Canadian five-dollar bill would be easy. Boy was I wrong.

*Simulacrum*, I mumble to my shoebox in the sky. *Word of the day*, my mother would have said way back when, and after some digging, I would have described a simulacrum as *an inferior representation of a person or thing, a hollow imitation*. I like the sound of that word.

Simulacrum.

I'm not sure why I'm creating this simulacrum, and on my first attempt, my freelancer Alex says there's a problem. An error notice from Photoshop because the software won't let him edit a banknote. The software is systemically racist. Alex isn't sure *how* it detects a Negro face – only that when he tries it with similar banknotes, he runs into the same problem.

Whether it only happens to Negro faces, or Caucasian ones too, he won't say. Instead, he suggests closing my order or reconsidering my concept. Maybe I could add my mother's Negro face to a different background altogether?

But I insist. She wants to be famous, and I love her, so it's the least I can do. A half-formed idea is rattling around inside my head, maybe a book, and the first rule of any journey is knowing where you're headed. That's especially true for a book: begin with the end in mind, whether that ending turns out happy, sad, or indifferent.

I reply to Alex with a screenshot of the Canadian five-dollar bill, a cartoonish question mark posted where Sir Wilfred Laurier's famously receding hairline should be. The page header reads:

Your nominations for the next $5 bank note

Put it *there*, on the question mark.

Online, plenty of phony banknotes are peddled as novelty items every day, so it must be possible. Coming soon: a victory for racial justice so minor no one will even notice. Let's hope we don't wind up in prison.

## 2. ONE LAST WAY TO GET BACK AT HER

Where to begin? With my mother's longstanding rivalry with the late Viola Desmond, of course. I rehearse as I approach my childhood home, knowing she'll wonder why I'm asking so many questions. But the questions are necessary, and secrecy is paramount.

To understand her Bell case, you need to first understand my mother. She can be *overinclusive*. That's the medical description we use for those who are generous with extraneous details, the gregarious patients who tell me not only what cardiologist they're seeing for their angina, but also what colour his eyes were, and that he looked like he hadn't slept in a solid month. Did the cardiologist have a brusque attitude? Not my business. Just the facts, ma'am.

My mother and I share DNA, but we're not the same. For example, she'd first insist that I describe her garden as I approach the house. On and on about how it's autumn, and the changing leaves cast her maple a fiery crimson set against the hash-browned remains of the front lawn. In fairness, one would be a source of pride to her, and the other, great shame.

A confession: I'm indifferent to both. The death of a large patch of her lawn causes my mother a despair I can't understand. In these leafy suburbs, lawns seem significant, but they were always impermanent, not so different from people. Forget the lawn. That a solitary elderly woman is managing this enormous house is the real victory, a spiteful thrust against the forces of entropy.

But that's impermanent too. Most things are.

Still, who would expect a seventy-seven-year-old Black woman to be living alone in this five-bedroom, detached home in the suburbs, with its meticulously weeded flowerbeds and manicured garden? Amazing how rarely she stops to appreciate that.

I'm proud of her. Not just for the garden. In my line of work, most people her age are profoundly broken in some way, and sometimes in all ways. Canes, walkers, visiting nurses, Meals on Wheels. If an eighty-year-old doesn't pick up the phone once, they might be on the toilet. Twice, and the ultimatums begin. The third time, an ambulance gets called. People assume something awful has happened, and they're usually right.

But when she opens the front door, my mother is the same as always, a picture of dignity frozen in time. A *doña*, Dominicans would call her. Her hair is grey and straight, because *naturalized African hair is for young people*, and she is wearing the azure cloth mask I bought her to celebrate year two of the pandemic. I can't see her mouth, but her eyes look happy to see me.

I follow her down the hallway and into the kitchen, and then begin my visit with a planned provocation.

"What do you think of this new ten-dollar bill?"

I dangle a crisp banknote lengthwise at eye level as she begins washing the dishes. It might as well be hanging from the end of a fishing line. Bait.

Viola Desmond's face is upright in clumsy portrait orientation. The banknote itself is brand new, fresh from the mint save for the wallet crease around her chin. I know perfectly well what my mother thinks of these ten-dollar bills. Viola is the first and only Black person to be immortalized on a Canadian bank note. My mother will be the second, but only if Alex pulls through.

"I don't like them," she answers. She turns off the faucet. "Why is her face sideways? It's very awkward. I think that was *racist*."

"Racist?" I say, amused. "It's a Black woman on a ten-dollar bill!"

"They put her face sideways on purpose to make her look stupid."

"One last way to get back at her?"

"Yeah. What did she do to make you think she deserves to be on the ten-dollar bill?"

"It wasn't my idea."

"All she did was sit down where she shouldn't have been sitting! One day of her life, an insult. She suffered for *one day*. Maybe in those days, people just obeyed, but--"

"--she heroically said *no*," I conclude. My mother laughs. Occasionally, she appreciates my sarcasm.

"People love a good fight," I continue, warming to my theme. "If the same thing happened today, no way would I give up my seat. I would have been indignant, fired up. What an adrenaline rush! And I'm supposed to be the meek one. If I wouldn't vacate my seat, then neither would you. And if *you* wouldn't, then any other Roberts in your family would have made them sorry they ever looked at that seat twice."

I stop short of suggesting she comes from a family of

angry Black women. But my point stands, or at least sits comfortably in the Whites Only section. Viola Desmond might have lived through a racist time, but children are reliably less racist than their parents. Things are better now, and they'll be even better in the future. They're so much better now that it would be stranger for a Black woman to quietly comply, than for her to react with the righteous anger so richly deserved.

I hate badgering my mother with this. But crossing the ocean on a raft is more remarkable than doing so in a Boeing. If only she'd concede times have changed.

# 3. ROLL OVER, ROSA

This is a story about a Canadian hero.

Viola Desmond was a middle-class businesswoman from early twentieth century Nova Scotia who travelled to New York, then New Jersey, and then Montreal in pursuit of a hairdressing degree. Eventually, she came home and opened a studio in Halifax called *Vi's Studio of Beauty Culture*. When

I first read her life story, it was alongside an old black and white photograph and my first thought was that she was half Black, but not half as Black as I expected.

I lean over the kitchen counter and pretend to read Viola's biography from my phone. Truth is, I've already read it several times and made detailed notes.

"In 1946 – nine years before Rosa Parks refused to sit in the coloured section of a bus in Montgomery, Alabama – Viola Desmond entered the whites-only section of the Roseland Theatre and refused to be relocated to the balcony designated for coloured people. She was confronted where she sat, arrested, and jailed overnight– setting the stage for a landmark human rights case in Canada."

"She was eventually convicted of failing to pay a penny in tax. But ultimately, she was posthumously pardoned by the Black lieutenant governor of Nova Scotia in 2010. She now has an eponymous ferry, a scholarship, a postage stamp bearing her name, and a star on Canada's Walk of Fame."

Not to mention her face on the ten-dollar bill I'm holding, although my mother is underwhelmed. She dries her hands with the dishcloth and faces me.

"Look at the *eight years* of garbage I put up with at Bell

Canada," she says. "Look at the results I gave them, the money in revenue I created for them. And they still would *not* recognize me, come hell or high water."

"What do you mean '*all the money you made for them*?'"

"All the sales!"

"You probably *cost* them money after you sued them," I point out. "You must have been a net loss once you factor in their high-priced legal team."

She pauses, like she can't decide whether to laugh or scold me. In the end, she chooses neither and presses on.

"They probably spent as much on their legal team as they would have paid me in the settlement," she admits. "I wonder where my file is now. I bet they're hoping none of it sees the light of day. They couldn't afford for that case to be heard. They hired *Heenan Blaikie* – the law firm Pierre Trudeau joined after he retired as Prime Minister. Trudeau should have known better."

"Isn't there something in the Bible about punishing the sins of the father?" I argue. "We've got Justin Trudeau now, and maybe he's a white devil too. Maybe he should take some of the blame."

"I wonder if he knows what kind of cases his father's

firm was taking on," my mother says. "When Pierre Trudeau died, Heenan stood up there and cried during his eulogy. And I watched, thinking *look at this hypocrite. People don't realize what a devil you are.* It was like having Donald Trump deliver a eulogy."

"I didn't see it."

"Christopher," she whispers, "there are hidden racists."

"But you vote for Trudeau," I protest, because I know she's been sending a decade worth of cheques directly to Hell. "You donate to his party."

"And he should apologize."

*Preposterous.* As if a sitting prime minister would apologize on behalf of a corporation. As if a corporation would apologize for something (as far as I know) still before the courts.

They're probably all the same doubts someone had about granting clemency to Viola Desmond, that is, before they nominated her face for immortality. No wonder my mother takes it personally. If Viola makes your currency, you could justify minting legal tender for anyone else who has wrestled adversity. You could make the case for a heroic banknote for every Canadian man, woman, and child – maybe even a phony five-dollar bill bearing my mother's face. If everyone's a hero, no one is.

Saying this out loud would provoke my mother's wrath, so I fold the ten-dollar note and return it to my wallet.

## 4. A MACAROON FOR THE HECTOROON

She's still in the kitchen, and so am I. I'm holding the strap of my canvas backpack because it's a quarter after three, time to go. Over the last few hours, the problem with Viola Desmond has crystallized for me, although my mother will disagree.

The problem is that Viola is a *usurper*. She isn't Black enough, but it's undiplomatic to say so in polite company. I rack my brain for the words to phrase it delicately.

"She's not Black enough, mom," I say. "Look at you. You're much Blacker than her."

That's tactless because I'm not sure who really *is* Black enough. For anything.

"Come on, Christopher," my mother answers. "One

drop of Black blood is enough to be Negro."

Is it? I'm fifty percent white, and that's a hundred percent her fault. Most African Americans, after four hundred years in the Americas, are mixed blood anyway, and their light skin is no genetic fluke. To find full-blooded Blacks the colour of shadow, you'd have to travel all the way to Africa herself, where their undiluted Blackness is only the most superficial of the differences with their erstwhile descendants an ocean away. Beyoncé would be as lost in the forests of Sierra Leone as Shania Twain.

In the United States, they dealt with inevitable race mixing by assigning the children of such unions to the social group with the lower status – in other words, the race of the Blackest parent. Depending on the state, one-eighth or even one-sixteenth blood was plenty Negro. Someone one quarter Black was known as a *quadroon*, someone one eighth Black a *hectoroon*, and one-sixteenth made a *hexadecaroon*. A small dessert cake made from ground almonds, coconuts, and sweetened condensed milk was known as a *macaroon*.

"You can look like almost anything and be Black," says my mother. "Blacks have always accepted people who don't look completely Black. When I was in university, I read a book called *Black Like Me* for one of my assignments. It's quite famous now. It's about a white man in the Deep South who dyed his face and body so that he would be accepted as a Black man. Then he lived the life of a Negro in 1959 and wrote about the experience."

This derails me. What could a white man in blackface have to contribute to understanding the Black experience? I try to imagine a white journalist today prancing about in black shoe polish, mimicking the stereotyped vernacular and vocal inflections of an African American, and then claiming he was acting in the name of social justice.

"Okay," I finally say, deciding that having heard the title, I need the book. "Even that synopsis sounds racist. You'd be cancelled forever if you tried that now. Remember how it was international news when someone leaked those photos of Justin Trudeau in blackface for his Arabian Nights party?"

"That was all for fun!"

Typical. Only an hour ago, she was attacking the elder Trudeau, and now she's defending the escapades of the younger.

"But did you mistake him for a Negro?" I ask, borrowing my mother's dusty anachronism.

"No, he looked *awful!*"

In other words, the first thing someone would notice about the junior Trudeau in blackface was that he looked like a white face in blackface. Turns out a Black face is more than just a skin colour, more than just a minstrel show.

"My point is that you're Blacker than Viola Desmond. She was just another light skinned mulatto like me," I insist, wielding another anachronism. No need to pull punches around family. "But maybe putting you on currency has nothing to do with your shade. Maybe you're just not Canadian enough for the five-dollar bill. Viola was born and raised in Nova Scotia. Maybe you need to be born here."

"What do you mean, *not Canadian enough*?" She snaps at the bait. "I've been here fifty years, Christopher."

She has a point, and my train will leave without me if I don't hurry. I sling my backpack onto my shoulder, and as I do, my phone vibrates. Alex.

## 5. THE NEXT BANK NOTE-ABLE CANADIAN

Success.

He added her image to another software program called *Illustrator*, saved it, then added it back to Photoshop. There's always a workaround. Honestly, no one's ever asked him to edit a banknote before, and he wasn't sure whether to report me to the police.

When I open the file, I find a floating image disconnected from any reality. A simulacrum. A monochromatic photograph of Lyris Dainton in her younger days, flanked by the architecture of the standard Canadian five-dollar bill. If I squint, I can imagine my own mother famous and celebrated in some mirror universe, the bold new face of racial justice.

Alex might be my first convert, because his chosen backdrop is the 2020 webpage for *"The next bank NOTE-able Canadian"*. Underneath that Photoshopped image, a bulleted paragraph reads:

Nominees must meet these basic criteria:

1. They are a Canadian by birth or naturalization who has demonstrated outstanding leadership, achievement, or distinction in any field, benefiting the people of Canada, or in the service of Canada.
2. They are not a fictional character.

I wonder which fictional characters have previously been nominated, and why the bank discriminates against them. And even if my mother were fictional, I doubt it would make her story any less relevant, nor any less resonant for thousands of immigrants in similar skin and shoes. It would still be truer than most things these days.

Inspired, I keep scanning the text. First, the Bank of Canada plans to hold public consultations on tens of thousands of half-baked submissions, which they would whittle to a long list of hundreds. What follows are public surveys of thousands of real Canadians. Then, an expert advisory council meets to develop a shortlist. Finally, multiple focus groups approve a handful of final nominees to be reviewed by the Minister of Finance.

In other words, it's hopeless. Hopeless, even before I stumble over the last obstacle:

3. They have been deceased for at least 25 years.

Twenty-five years: long enough to protect the legacy of the nominees from any Twitter-related indiscretions. No chance to displace Viola Desmond for at least half a generation. The next shortlist will be Indigenous, with perhaps a token Terry Fox-type thrown in as a nod to the obsolete white male. One day, our currency will be a gender diverse, multiracial mosaic. But even in this golden age for reconciliation, lightning never strikes twice. We already have our immortal Black woman, and it's Viola Desmond of Nova Scotia.

There's just no room for another.

There's no room for my mother.

## 6.  BLACK ENOUGH

If anyone can complain that Viola Desmond isn't Black enough, it's me, an ethnically ambiguous mulatto from the suburbs of Toronto. Not being Black enough is a sore spot, and I eventually gave up. If Viola gave up too, then it's no wonder she tried her luck in the whites only section.

An old girlfriend once introduced me to her close Black friend, part-time deejay, and full-time Michael. Noticing that most of her close friends were Black, Michael had become adamant that she needed to get over herself and round out her experience by dating a few good Black men. When I met him for the first time, he was tinkering behind a sophisticated sound system, blasting Soca beats all over his private beach party, which everyone would agree is a decisively Black exercise. But Soca makes me uncomfortable, evinces an apologetic awkwardness for not speaking, gesturing, nor carrying myself the way an authentic Black man should. The booming rhythm left me unsure whether I should sit or stand, let alone where to put my limbs, and when my then-girlfriend boasted that she'd finally taken his advice, Michael aptly roasted her for having chosen *the whitest Black guy*.

Bullseye.

Leaving aside my own sensitivities, anyone with eyes and ears would admit that I'm not Black enough, that I haven't exercised that muscle nearly enough. These suburbs are too leafy for that, and the number of Blacks in my high school classrooms could usually be counted on one finger. But I've never been white enough either; the *one drop* rule takes care of that. I can tell good roti and doubles from bad, and in adulthood, that usually gives me a pass.

When I reach my downtown shoebox, I pick up the phone to ask an Indian what it's like to be Black.

"Is it more like being a Muslim, an Arab, or a Jew?"

"Let me think about it," says Avani, a model minority. Pocket-sized, charismatic, fiercely intelligent. "Maybe somewhere in the middle. If I swap out Black for Indian, it doesn't quite work."

"A Muslim has to pray in the right direction," I say as she muses. "An Arab just *looks* like one, like it or not. And an ethnic Jew is Jewish even if they're invisible or self-hating, even if they pretend not to be one. Anti-Semites don't care how you perceive yourself."

"Why are you asking?"

"Because I could be blacker."

"Like, physically darker? Yes."

"I could listen to more Soca and wear my pants lower."

"True."

"Eat more fried chicken and watermelon?"

"Those are just American stereotypes."

"True." What does it mean to be properly Black? Maybe it's like being a chair. You just know a good chair when you see one.

"Then what do you call a white person who fits those stereotypes?"

"Not Black, that's for sure," I answer. "Maybe blackness begins with some Black blood. Necessary, but not sufficient. And after that, you still need to fill out the application at the Ministry of Blackness and wait six to eight weeks for review and approval."

It isn't a perfect analogy. The darker the pigment, the harder it becomes to claim someone isn't Black enough, and we can't all be *Abagbe Adebayo* either in name or appearance. But there's no denying that growing up in the leafy suburbs creates tribalism amongst the scattered minorities. They cling together like grains of salt in a cooling beaker, and as with all tribes, each develops its own subculture. In the mid-nineties, the Black tribe in my high school borrowed theirs from the Americans, stole their role models exclusively from the worlds of basketball and hip hop.

They. We.

We cribbed the clothing, the music, and the vocal inflections. We became disciples of *gangsta rap* and its high clerics Tupac Shakur and Biggie Smalls, and exacted a social penalty for academic achievement, that conspicuous mark of otherness that didn't fit the expected identity for a young, Black male.

We? They.

I'd always found it strange for Black teenagers from the suburbs to sound any more like American rappers than suburban whites should sound like British lords. But that didn't stop us (them?) from trying, from substituting American for Canadian history as if the two were interchangeable, from importing a certain manner of thinking about ourselves and then dragging that identity around with us like baggage. I cringe when I recall my own performative Blackness phase, back when my mother forced me to overdub the explicit lyrics on Snoop Dogg's *Doggystyle* album. Chopped and mutilated, not much remained of that cassette afterwards.

Avani finishes reflecting.

"There's this…interchange between culture, race, ethnicity, and nationality," she begins. "Nobody gets the nuances of Black culture. And the speed it's evolving and becoming global is defying our ability to say what it is. Maybe *Black* is anything you want it to be.

"And people have these intense opinions about it, especially if you're Black and you're defining it for yourself. No one even scrutinizes it, because questioning a Black person's blackness is basically signing your own social media death warrant. Maybe it's just a mix of everything."

I'm impressed. That was profound.

Of course, in the real world, none of that worked for me. I was cast out from the tribe like a leper, excluded from the lone Black lunch table in the cafeteria. My closest adult friends are a multiracial jambalaya of mostly model minorities like Avani and a conspicuous absence of Blacks.

There are concrete ways I could work to be Blacker – invest in the hair, lean into the culture, surround myself with the right people. But my Black single mother worked hard to make it to these leafy suburbs and leave me in identity's sweet spot. Black privilege – maybe she wanted exactly this, a mulatto just the right shade to rob less fortunate Blacks of their opportunities whenever it becomes convenient, a macaroon with just the right mannerisms to pass for Caucasian in the white company.

The *right* company.

Maybe I should feel guilty about that.

# 7. FUNERALS ARE FOR THE LIVING

It takes a funeral to make people think about death. My second visit to the suburbs in as many weeks comes when Neil Herbert Clifton Junior dies of Covid.

Twin cloth masks again when I reach the door. She hugs me, and I hesitate before returning the gesture. *There's a pandemic*, my mother reminds me, as though I could forget. She's cautious enough to insist on masks inside her home, although not cautious enough to banish me. Each of us is the other's only family here, and banishment feels cruel.

One doesn't go to a funeral so much as logs onto one these days, and as a peak millennial, tech support falls to me. Having propped the laptop on the kitchen table, I slide two wooden chairs sideways and surrender the front row seat to my mother. When the livestream appears, we drop in on a perfectly Southern funeral unfolding in a church on the outskirts of Atlanta. My mother perches, heron-like over the screen, carefully inspecting the well-dressed screen people in attendance. Funerals are for the living.

Funerals make me realize that my mother, too, is old now, and she won't be around forever. One day, the dreaded, inevitable phone call: *Are you Lyris Dainton's son? You should come to the hospital now. Your mother is extremely sick.* I make those phone calls from the Emergency Room. *Extremely sick* is a euphemism for *nearly dead*.

"I don't think it's a Catholic funeral," complains my mother. "I'll be very upset if I don't see a Catholic priest."

"Was Neil even Catholic?" I say stubbornly, as if that matters, which it doesn't. Funerals are for the living.

It's a congregation of segregation, because that never died in Georgia. All two dozen screen people are Black, weaves and bald heads lined up like rosary beads along the pews. Neil Junior's wife is Black, as are his friends, his wife's friends, and anybody else who meant enough to merit an invitation to this intimate gathering. He never got kicked out of the cafeteria lunch table.

To my mother's chagrin, the preacher is no Catholic. Lord, no.

I'm relieved to be a screen away: family reunions are one of those places I'm not Black enough to be. My skin is too light, my features too sharp. Alone, that's forgivable – except my accent is all wrong, in all the ways an accent can be wrong. My voice doesn't resonate enough, my vocal inflections hopelessly Canadian to my own ear. The sound of a colour should be an incoherent concept, but it's not. Over the phone, you could never guess my pigment.

A wave of guilt washes over me when I acknowledge that Neil's funeral intimidates me. But then again, the dead don't carry grudges, so any old way I feel about the sound of my Blackness is perfectly fine with Neil Junior. Funerals are for the living.

The preacher begins. The repetition and melodrama of his cadence tell me that he's none other than Baptist.

"Even when we don't understand, Lord, we trust you. We come, Lord, with tears in our eyes, and yet the understanding that we trust You. We give You glory even when we don't understand, and know You are there with us. We celebrate the life of Neil, family man, husband, father, man of God. Servant to his friends and his family. We come to honour his life."

When he finishes, a gospel singer and a keyboard take over.

"I'm so upset by the world in general," my mother says during the interlude, eyes transfixed by the screen. "My friends are dying or being mistreated in old folks' homes. You and I, we're alone in this world. Is this what's going to happen to us?"

"That's what happens to everyone," I say.

We're like lawns.

"It's frightening."

"Can be."

"Look how cold you are about it."

"I don't mean to be."

"You were cold when I told you how my friend has no phone in her room in the nursing home, and that when she speaks, nobody can understand."

"Mmmhmm."

"Bernice is eighty-five," she continues. "She's ready to die, any day. She's made her peace with God. I'm ready too, any day. I only hope my soul is pleasing enough to get to purgatory, where any stains will be burned off."

That's not true. She's not ready. If she were ready, she wouldn't insist on these masks. Everybody is terrified, and nobody is ready. I turn back to the screen, where another man has stepped up to the podium. Another white collar mounted on a black suit.

"The Lord is my shepherd," says this one.

"That's right," agrees one of the screen people.

"He maketh me lie down in green pastures."

"Yes."

"He restores my soul."

"Read the book, preacher, read."

"He leadeth me in the path of righteousness for His namesake."

"Read the book."

Call and response, a hypnotic rhythm to his pregnant pauses, punctuated by spontaneous rejoinders from the mourners. Before long, the first preacher nudges him aside again.

"Lord, we say *thank you* because there are some things we won't know until we come into Your presence. *Thank you* for a mother who never thought she would lay her son down to rest before he would do so for her, and yet she can give You praise because she knows she lays him into Your hands."

"Thank you," agrees one of the screen people.

Call and response. It isn't how any funeral in Toronto would play out, but Georgians would find our customs equally strange. *People walk different here*, declared another cousin upon arriving in downtown Toronto for a family reunion, inspecting my northern habitat the way a colonial anthropologist might inspect island natives in the South Pacific. My cousin spoke how you'd expect a young Black American to speak, and he walked how you'd expect a young Black American to walk. *What you'd expect* depends on your own prejudices, or maybe on mine.

When he left, we never spoke again.

## 8. THE EULOGY

"In the twinkle of an eye, we will all be in your presence," says the preacher.

And then my cousin Curtis replaces him at the pulpit, an imposing physical presence even without his police uniform. Curtis is the only Roberts currently married to a white woman, but not the only Roberts *ever* married to a white woman. This makes perfect sense for a devout Black Republican. Or else, being a devout Black Republican makes perfect sense after marrying a Southern white woman.

"Brother Neil was a lot of things," Curtis begins. Smiles. "A jokester. He talked me into getting into a clothes dryer when we were children. I'm still dizzy. Neil always took care of his friends and his family. He could have a conversation and disagree, but it would still be a great conversation. He'd say: *Well alright, I love you, keep your head down.* I miss that already."

His voice breaks, but only for a moment.

"So many times, I'd cook something on the grill and call him up. Just this weekend, I barbequed some ribs on my new grill, and I couldn't wait to rub it in his face. I hope that's not why he passed, because he didn't want to try them. He lived his life for this moment, for the ones that were here."

That was Neil's story, his legacy. Making good ribs was his chosen approach to life and living, and he died the way he lived. He wasn't a small man, but good ribs will do that.

No one gains immortality through their succulent, mouth-watering ribs, nor preserves those ribs in amber for the appreciation of future generations. Funerals are for the living, and the not-dead-yet like a good eulogy to remind them that one day, their lives might deserve the same.

Maybe it's vanity to feel compelled to persist beyond ribs. Neil never worried about life after death, and words like *closure* and *legacy* hardly matter amid the deafening silence of the universe. On the other hand, my mother doesn't find the idea of closure to be absurd, and without it, part of me wonders if she plans to haunt a certain telephone company.

"I guess that's it for Neil Junior," I announce to my mother as Curtis steps down. Hollow words. Viola might have made a mean rack of ribs too. As it stands, she exists only as a parable, although somehow it matters that her story is no fiction. It matters that she was true flesh and blood once, rather than invented mythology. It matters that her story happened here, rather than Middle Earth or Bora Bora.

People are awed by truth, by true stories that have – by some miraculous stroke of luck – closure in the same way fiction has a beginning, a middle, and an end. But right now, my mother's story only has a beginning and a middle. I need it to have an end.

## 9. THE NEGRO IN AMERICA

"Mom, I need all your stuff."

Her eyes narrow. "You know where to find it," she says, before adding: "What do you need it for?"

"I don't know." I turn and march upstairs to the hall closet, backpack slung over my shoulder. She's right. I know exactly where to find it.

Top to bottom, the shelves are obsessively, impeccably organized. Musty, like a used bookstore. At the top, an eclectic array of rejected bath towels – creamy white, coffee brown, lime green, and cherry red. The shelf below holds bundled tax files in yellowed envelopes, meticulously labelled by date, and beside them, stacks of elementary school report cards.

Crouching, I set upon a neatly piled collection of photo albums, university assignments, and correspondence from a generation ago. The sort of priceless collection that, were the house to spontaneously burst into flames, one's priority would be to seize a heaping armful of nostalgia before diving shoulder-first through an upstairs window.

I find what I'm looking for in a matter of seconds: a thick folder overstuffed with newspaper clippings, stapled documents, and photocopies. A synopsis of my mother's case against Bell Canada. The abbreviated version, the go-pack, the one she would share with acquaintances with short attention spans and dubious curiosity that wouldn't withstand wading through a muck of legal procedurals.

I slide the folder into my backpack. Easier to ask forgiveness than permission.

Something else is concealed beneath that folder. A typewritten manuscript of loose-leaf pages peeking through a battered transparent plastic folder, the type of presentation portfolio that elementary school students used to be enormously proud of before email rendered them obsolete.

The title page reads:

The Negro in the United States
By Lyris Roberts
Submitted to Reverend Alan MacDonald

Submitted in October 1962, to be exact. A sociology term essay. Its first two pages are frayed, but the timeworn paper is in otherwise good condition, edges scarcely tinged with yellow. In blue ink beside the title, the Reverend has awarded my mother an 'A', and scrawled an encouraging message of praise underneath:

"*Good.*"

I imagine myself in the Reverend's shoes. In my mind's eye, he's a sepia caricature wrapped in a dowdy tweed jacket, a standard accessory of the oversized oak desk in an old-fashioned study whose walls are adorned with antique wainscotting and leatherbound English literature. He plucks an essay from his stack and finds himself grading a manuscript about the plight of the American Negro, written by one of the only two Black students in the entire university.

Awkward. Maybe folks back then didn't worry about

being branded bigots or violating safe spaces. But whatever the sensibilities of the time, *Good* was the safest reaction he dared commit to ink.

I flip to the second page.

The problem of the negro in the United States is much like that in South Africa, with the important difference that while one seems to be heading towards improvement, the other is rapidly worsening.

A good point. No doubt about it.

I can't decide which problem was improving and which was worsening. Must have been the United States, because only yesterday, an Indian colleague complained to me that *nothing is getting better*, neither down there nor up here.

Plenty of model minorities in the medical profession, and as one such model minority, he was furious. The anti-Black rot was endemic, corrupting every institution. I'm always on the wrong side of these conversations, I decided. Too much trouble to disagree – to point out I'm doing just fine as a Black emergency doctor, thank you, other than the rare racial epithet from the mouth of patients profoundly altered by drugs, and one woman who complained that *all the psychiatrists are Black, and none of them speak proper English.* Too much trouble to disagree, so I made some agreeable sounds before leaving my colleague to simmer.

Nevertheless, here is my own revolutionary mother terrifying the white establishment of the civil rights era.

Here, the word *negro* is raw, uncapitalized, and subversive. It didn't earn capitalization until the turn of the twentieth century, the same way *black* men grew into *Black* men after the murder of George Floyd a century later. Derek Chauvin's knee put pressure on race relations, squeezed another noble loop onto the small b, made it less pointy. Journalism decided the small-b was disgraceful, negated the shared community of the Black hive-mind.

*White* isn't a culture, just a skin colour. When ethnicity matters, journalists ask directly about Italian-*ness*, Russian-*ness*, Ukrainian-*ness*. Blackness, in contrast, must be as homogenous as a cauldron of bats, a huddled mass of interchangeable black bodies without uniqueness. But if Caribbean Blacks, African Blacks and American Blacks share a universal culture, it's news to many of them, since Black people only seem alike to white eyes. There's only a grain of truth in that capital B: the instinctive purity test for who qualifies as Black enough, and who's sold out.

It's taboo driving language – the rise and fall of euphemisms that dodge their offensive cousins before becoming inevitably ensnared by their real meaning. Then, a new euphemism appears on the scene: American Indians, Aboriginals, Indigenous, First Nations People, a treadmill of evolving linguistic symbols representing the same concept. Noises we make to communicate our intentions.

I plunge deeper into my mother's manifesto. Prejudice is contagious, she says, spread by older playmates, community leaders, and especially by parents. But it wasn't always that way. White Europeans and negroes even intermarried in Virginia before slavery became the established norm. Children are innocent, she says, and racism is far from innate.

If true, that's *good* too. The Reverend must have thought so in the 1960s, contemplating his privilege at that sepia desk in that sepia room.

But I don't buy the innocence of children. Neither does Abagbe Adebayo, who claims children are tiny sociopaths. *Children take things that don't belong to them, throw tantrums, and behave irrationally. Why should we be surprised that they gravitate towards people who look like them?*

If anyone deserves a hot take on race, it's him. Abagbe Adebayo is the blackest person I know.

# 10. MISCEGENATION FOR BEGINNERS

I wonder if my mother ever asked one of her ex-boyfriends to proofread her essay for content, flow, and grammar.

If so, Ron (or Leon) would have encountered the following:

In the United States, twenty-nine Southern and Western states have laws against marriage between negroes and whites. There is a strong feeling against miscegenation in any form, since the purity of the white race is violated by sexual contact with the negro in or out of marriage. The child of a negro-white union automatically becomes a negro. The negro who passes as white no longer presents any contradiction to the eyes of others, but he still has the inner dilemma.

Grammatically flawless, and its content deemed *good*, Ron (or Leon) would have hastily returned the paper, changed the subject, and wiped his perspiring pink hands on his trousers.

I look up *miscegenation*, a word as close to a fossilized artifact as someone is liable to find in any dictionary. *Interbreeding of different people considered to be of different racial types.* In modern Canada, where everyone is a progressive global citizen, that's more commonly known as *dating*.

Into the backpack goes *The Negro in the United States*, spiritual companion to the Bell Canada dossier beside it. I march back downstairs.

## 11. THAT WHICH CAN NEVER DIE

"What is it you want from Bell?"

"Christopher, are you writing a book about this?" A deflection. "You never tell me what you're working on. I never keep secrets from you. I tell you what's happening from the *bottom of my heart.*"

"What is it you want from Bell?" I insist.

"Well, I still want that case completed. It was just… abandoned."

"Completed how?"

"Completed to my satisfaction as a settlement. Completed to compensate me for the five years it took to find another job. All that lost salary, lost benefits, lost retirement income, and all the interest on it. When I walked away from that case, it was worth at least a million dollars. In 1985, a million dollars was a lot of money."

"It's still a lot of money now."

A good compromise leaves both sides equally miserable. And adequate compensation should make a person precisely whole, no more and no less. Justly compensated, the victim neither celebrates nor regrets having suffered their experience.

"So, a million dollars, adjusted for inflation."

"Yes, Christopher."

"What if they apologized? Publicly or privately acknowledged wrongdoing, shook your hand, and gave you a commemorative plaque?"

"Anybody can apologize and not mean it. *Sorry* doesn't cut it. Somebody should open that case again or file a class action suit. I've even thought about calling Mary Eberts."

"Isn't she dead?"

"No, she's still alive and active. She was such a champion for me. Every time we appeared in court, she'd say: *they're waiting for you and me both to die, and for our witnesses to die or be spread out all over the world.*"

"If you picked up the case again and fought them another nine years, you'd be eighty-five when you win."

Victory enough if my mother outlives all her former persecutors. All but one, whom through the authority of Canada's Corporations Act, has no fleshy heart, body, or soul, and cannot die without the submission of formal articles of dissolution. That persecutor is Bell Canada, which shines eternal, like the sun, the moon, and the stars.

"When I look at those files in the basement," continues my mother, "it gives me high blood pressure. I still remember what they put me through, the pain of living through it." She shakes her head. "Bell must have laughed their heads off when I stopped bothering them."

"Bell isn't a person," I point out. "A corporation doesn't have any heads."

I imagine a well-lit boardroom whose floor-to-ceiling

windows overlook Toronto's glass and concrete monoliths, a gleaming mahogany plank besieged by two dozen middle-aged white villains in plain suits, each face plainer than the last, each interchangeable man holding a champagne flute. They're cackling, naturally. Toasting business as usual.

Maybe that's far-fetched. Maybe, Bell Canada is no more a villain than a lawnmower that amputates the groundskeeper's fingers.

"Back then," says my mother, "so many Black women went through things like this. Bernice went through it in the sixties when she came from Jamaica. It still burns her when she thinks about how she was treated. They wouldn't give her a job for three years."

They.

"But I don't have the energy to fight Bell again on my own," she continues. "I couldn't take it. My chest tightens and my pressure goes up. My youth is gone. If only there were someone younger."

## 12. YEOMAN'S WORK

"You should try the Google," she suggests. "It's fascinating to read about the case. If it went back to court now, they wouldn't have a leg to stand on. Just thinking about what they did brings back so many indignities. I carry them with me every day, and it hurts my heart."

But any trace of a human rights case against Canada's then telecommunications monopoly has vanished from the historical record.

*Bell Canada. Lyris Dainton. Racism. Human rights. Nothing. It looks like there aren't many great matches for your search*, complains the search engine that can still find twenty-year-old letters to my university newspaper.

"Bell Canada and racial discrimination," I say, announcing my latest attempt as I punch in the words and scan the meagre output. "They're doing yeoman's work, mom."

"What's a yeoman?"

"It's the word of the day. Someone who performs a great and loyal service. It looks like Bell's loyal service is its tireless commitment to amplifying voices in the fight against racism."

I hand over my phone. She squints to decipher the hopelessly tiny text.

> Bell Media is committed to engaging Canadians in a conversation about the racism and social injustice that exist in our country," said Randy Lennox, President, Bell Media. "Change is never easy, but it's the uncomfortable conversations that ultimately lead to action.

"That's it?" she gingerly hands the phone back to me, cradling it like a priceless Fabergé egg.

"That's it."

"Who's Randy?"

"He's nobody."

"What if you Google that human rights magazine?"

"Nothing. I mean, except more evidence that Bell Canada is pulling out all the stops to fight racism."

"Nine years of my life, and there's nothing on the Google? So many people wrote about it passionately back then. Maybe they paid somebody to take it off the internet."

"Maybe," I say. "All I can find is an archived report called '*Black woman going nowhere with Bell Canada*', but I can't even access that. Maybe the library has it on microfiche somewhere. Apparently, you can find anything on the internet, except this."

My mother frowns.

"Microfiche?"

## 13. LETTERS TO SANTA

The train home is sparsely populated with tense foreheads and blank faces wrapped in cloth and surgical masks. Pandemic, year two, perhaps staring down the barrel of an autumn wave of contagion.

I don't have any better idea now than before of what happened forty years ago, when I was a toddler, nor how much of my mother's version of history is accurate. I'm a sceptic. Everyone does their best with the truth, but sometimes the dress you experience as navy blue, I see as dusky grey. Neither of us is *lying*, because lying is something malicious and intentional. But one of us still needs their eyes checked.

Forty years have passed, and my mother's story is warped by time, perception, and bias, as if passed through a maze of funhouse mirrors. Sometimes, experiences can be confirmed by facts or testimony. But where do I look for truth now, when her ordeal has the musty scent of a cold case?

But Bell Canada is no ordinary lawnmower. It's a sentient machine with the unsettling audacity to publicly fight for racial justice while burying its own case with the Human Rights Tribunal, burying a body that's still warm. The human villains might be long gone, but the inhuman machine hasn't bothered to make anything right. My mother is still alive, and Bell Canada remains the schoolyard bully who crammed her into a locker – she's still *in that locker* while someone named Randy scolds the morning assembly about the scourge of bullying among students today.

Either way, I'm hooked.

None of this is Randy's fault, whoever he is. This president of Bell Media is as much a stranger to me as my mother is to him. His conscience isn't wrestling with this, and I'm the only living person motivated to point out the contradiction. I want to believe in Randy, who's shown uncommon willingness to engage in *uncomfortable conversations that lead to action*. But Randy didn't get where he is by clacking away at unsolicited emails from the public-at-large.

So, I start with Jessica and Mike, two of the few people in my social circle who exchange their talents for paycheques from large, faceless corporations. The first, a quirky Asian financial advisor, full-time cynic and part-time hipster musician; the second, a ruthlessly effective corporate negotiator with a head for realpolitik. Overpriced, oversized tee-shirts versus overpriced velvet hoodies. Designer jeans, both.

I start with Mike. I pick up my phone and unleash a flurry of messages. What happens to letters addressed to the CEO of a major corporation? That's Mirco Bibic, it looks like. Would addressing a letter directly to Mirco be any more effective than addressing it to Santa Claus? Maybe he'll forward it to somebody who cares.

"Mirco doesn't care what you think," says Mike.

"Yes, true," I say. "That's how I feel about voting in elections, that somehow, it's all for nothing. But I do it anyway."

Because it's symbolic. A letter to Mirco, in its magnificent and desperate futility, would be a beautiful gesture of engagement with an indifferent world. Like casting a message in a bottle out into the oblivion of the ocean, it represents heartfelt sentiment and the modest effort to make those feelings coherent. Much like a single vote among millions.

But Mike isn't a romantic.

"Exactly," he agrees. "Neither matter. Both are futile and insignificant."

# 14. SIPS AND CYNICISM

I meet Jessica for coffee the next day. A tuque covers her head, and her body is inflated by a too-big black and white parka, slight overkill for the weather.

Save for the plexiglass barriers that shield the baristas from their customers, it would be impossible to conclude from this café that the world was any different from a year ago. Jessica cradles her paper cup tightly in her hands, gazing down at the floating teabag as I explain what I plan to do. Then she looks up, clucks humourlessly, and hesitates before responding.

"Are you for real?" she asks. "You're really writing to Bell Canada? Are you really that bored?"

"Sure, why not?" I insist. "Where does a letter like this go after I hand it to the secretary?"

"The trash," she says. She seems genuinely angry about the letter's mere existence. Her own life is too busy for such trivial nonsense.

"Right away?"

"First of all," she continues, now laughing, "secretaries don't exist anymore. And second, no one is stupid enough to try to push a lawsuit that way. If you've been alive and watched any movie or television show, you know you get a lawyer. It's common sense. If you think a regular person walks into a large company with a letter that they wrote themselves about a cold case from forty years ago…"

"I don't think it's obvious outside the corporate world," I say, crossing my arms over my chest. Not everybody can afford a lawyer. Even if they could, most people don't have the time or energy to deal with the courts. Mostly, I want my letter to slightly irritate somebody, to burden them with some fleeting cognitive dissonance for the nanosecond before they ball it up and bin it. But I know she's right: without a lawyer's signature, they won't take it seriously. It might as well be written in crayon, covered in glitter, and decorated with pipe cleaners.

"Come on," says Jessica. She sips her tea. "Companies deal with petty lawsuits like this all the time, and most of them are more pressing than this one. Tons of people literally make a living off suing companies, and it looks like that's what you're doing."

I'm already dejected, but she twists the knife. The problem being a cynic is that all your friends are cynics too.

"Nothing means anything to a corporation unless there's an obvious consequence attached. Racism is easy to deny because there's never any physical proof."

Sounds like what I've been saying for years. But that's not what *Randy* is saying, I protest. Whoever he is.

"It might go to an assistant and then get put in a pile," she concedes. "You won't be called in to speak with anyone in person or anything. Maybe you get a boilerplate letter in a few months. But most likely, no response at all."

I finally sip my espresso. By now, it's bitter and cold. I forgot to add any sugar.

# 15. FORTRESS BELL

It's nice to get physical letters. Postcards, love letters, seasons greetings. Even nicer when they're hand delivered, which saves a postage stamp. My letter isn't quite as festive as a Christmas card, but it's holiday ready.

I proofread it one last time:

Dear Mirco Bibic,

I would like to inquire as to the status of Lyris Dainton's Human Rights case, opened in 1983 and alleging racism on the part of Bell Canada with regards to its hiring and promotion of employees.

Specifically, I wish to know if Bell Canada would be willing to settle this case by apologizing without reservation for its actions in the 1980s, and offering substantive compensation to the complainant, my mother Lyris Dainton.

> Amid the growing Black Lives Matter movement and increasing recognition of the legacy of systemic racism, both past and present, it occurred to me that this would be an excellent moment for Bell Canada to step up in its stated commitment to racial harmony, in a manner that is more than merely symbolic. I earnestly await your response.

It's hopeless and perfect. Perfectly hopeless, because if Mirco Bibic read letters from John Q. Public, it would be his only job.

My dress code in the emergency department amounts to a pair of the tattered blue pyjamas commonly known as scrubs, but today is no workday. Today, my introduction to the corporate world calls for a smart button-up shirt, charcoal grey dress-casual pants, and buffed leather shoes whose soles make a satisfying and hoof-like clop with every step.

First, I visit an office supply store to print two copies of my missive on heavy letterhead paper advertised as a *classic choice for elegant resumés, correspondence, and reports*. Its feel is substantial and legal when I run my fingers over the grain. With some trepidation, I make my way down Yonge Street, west on Adelaide, manila envelope in hand.

Bell Canada headquarters is a sleek, slate grey monstrosity, clad in marble around its front doors and steel surrounding its windows. Its blinds are drawn, eyes closed, building locked down like a fortress as if the corporation itself could contract the coronavirus. Entrance secured; revolving door cordoned off with yellow tape.

*Employees need authorization to enter*, reminds a notice posted next to the adjacent service door.

I find an intercom attached to a marble slab, and its companion button just underneath. I buzz and wait. Although I can see the moving form of a security guard beneath the crack of the blinds, several eons pass before his muffled voice crackles on the other side.

"Open the door," he says, buzzing me in.

I obey and find myself in a claustrophobic hallway with another secure door at the end. It resembles many things: an apartment foyer, the airlock of a space station, a decontamination zone within which visitors are aggressively hosed with disinfectant.

The guard sits behind the plexiglass barrier to my left. He's a chubby cherub on display in a transparent habitat box, a Black man wearing glasses.

"Can I help you?" His thick Caribbean accent reminds me of distant Trini relatives, and his expression wobbles between inscrutable and bored.

"I've got a letter for the Bell Canada head office," I say. "I'm guessing that legal is the best place for it. My friend and I have a bet. She thinks this letter goes directly in the garbage, but I think it makes it all the way to legal, and *then* the garbage."

"Hang on."

The security guard picks up the phone at his desk. I hear the rumble of his mumble behind the plexiglass, until he nods and hangs up.

"Sir, we don't accept this." He stares at me blankly through the two panes that separate us.

"You don't?"

"I was advised that we don't accept that letter, so I don't know."

"Then how do I get it to the legal department?"

"You have to go online."

"Do you know what the website is?"

"Bell Canada."

I can't tell if he genuinely believes this is helpful, or whether he is being intentionally dismissive.

"Why can't you take it in person? I mean, I'm already here."

"We don't accept this. We don't accept this, and that's it."

A second security guard trots up to the airlock's glass barrier. This one is slim, unshaven, and Indian. He's agitated, his bony arms folded across his chest like the lid covering a bursting pot of popcorn.

"We don't accept anything, sir," he says roughly. "Plain and simple. Take your package and leave right now."

*Or what*, I want to say. His tone is the kind that inspires fighting words in more emotional people. He has the diplomatic tact of a nightclub bouncer, without the imposing physique.

I swallow my pride and feign ignorance.

"I don't understand."

"What don't you understand?" he scowls, stepping in place like somebody who is quite itchy.

"Your tone," I say. "I'm just asking for a little help getting a letter to the right place."

"That's not our problem."

I retreat. As I do, it registers that this narrow hallway is neither an airlock nor a decontamination zone. It is a castle gatehouse, always the most heavily defended part of a medieval fortress, because it represents the most vulnerable target for an enemy. A classic gatehouse is usually rigged with a portcullis, arrow loops, and murder-holes through which boiling acid can be poured to foil would-be attackers.

Fortress Bell Canada has done away with the most barbaric of these indignities, I hope. No murder holes, but if either of them is packing a taser, I think it's the agitated one. I don't stay long enough to find out.

# 16. BLACKFACE AND BLACK FACES

Third visit. I arrive in these sullen suburbs on an overcast November morning, still stinging from my experience at the Bell head office, my pathetic letter impotently tucked inside my backpack. *Pathetic fallacy*: more than a solitary word for today, but still an apt literary description for the attribution of human emotion to the inhuman elements of nature.

This third visit, I'm keeping a promise to my mother

and come bearing an artifact. Not a fake banknote, but a tiny book delivered from the Amazon – the same one she referenced on my last visit. When it arrived in the mail, I devoured it cover to cover in under a day. Now, I vomit it back up, from my satchel onto the kitchen counter.

*Black Like Me*, by John Howard Griffin.

The groundbreaking true story of a white man who lived in blackface for several months in the 1950s, then wrote a book explaining to white folks what life was like wearing black skin. Possibly the most fascinating and audacious example of *whitesplaining* that I've encountered – and as entertained as I was, I mostly can't decide how his experiment was different from any other white man or prime minister smearing his face in shoe polish.

"So," I say, "you read this book when you were a student in Prince Edward Island."

"You found it!" Her face lights up as she runs her fingers across the pebbled cover, tracing the silhouette of a black man in profile, devoid of identifying features. She looks overjoyed, as if I personally exhumed the book from history's graveyard. "They were such wonderful people in Prince Edward Island, small town folks. I had such a time there."

"Wonderful white people," I add. "And they *weren't* racist? Because that's not what *Black Like Me* wants you to believe."

I can't guess her response. This is my mother, weary veteran of racial oppression – her spirit whittled down by the whims and vagaries of a catalogue of white devils. And we've now read the same book, a mere sixty years apart. Two eras, two perspectives.

"What did you think when you read it?"

"That it was fake," I say, diving in with passion. "He wants us to believe his blackface was more convincing than Justin Trudeau's. But back in the days of Jim Crow, I bet most white folks had *no idea* how a Negro was supposed to look, talk, and act. No one spent enough time outside their bubbles to understand how to pretend to be Black. If a white man approached you with his face smeared in shoe polish and claimed he was Jamaican, wouldn't you think you were being pranked?"

Because we recognize white people by not only by their skin colour, but by their manners, their accents, and their posture.

"You think he made this up?" My mother frowns. "I don't think that crossed *anybody's* mind. People were naïve back then. It's only now that the world is so wicked that people are sceptical about everything."

"I can't say for sure," I concede. "I just wonder how convincing his blackface would have been."

"What gives a Negro away is the flat nose," says my mother, adopting my anachronism. "But your cousin Curtis has Chinese eyes. That's what happens if you get a Negro who's taken bits from other races. Maybe that's why nobody noticed he was white. Like, *your* nose is straight. You could be a white, tanned person, you know."

"Right. But my face is real." I pause, surprised by this good point. "Still, good chance he looked freakish, like a caricature. Just so many layers to peel back. He'd have to *look* Black enough, and then *sound* Black enough, and then suppress the self-consciousness I assume he'd feel impersonating a Black man."

My mother nods. Times have changed. You can't get away with anything anymore – not when it comes to race.

"A Jewish liberal arts professor in the United States did something like that a while ago. Pretended to be Caribbean-Black to give herself some street cred with her students." I stop to find the article on my phone. "They didn't like it. Looks like she apologized and said she was *wrong, unethical, immoral, and colonial. I am not a culture vulture*, she wrote. *I am a culture leech.*"

I stop reading and scan the rest of the article, hoping for guidance on which impersonations should offend us. "Her students were shocked her entire academic life was a complete lie."

"Disgusting," my mother agrees. "Just awful."

# 17. THAT RING OF TRUTHINESS

Tepid autumn light haunts the kitchen windows. My mother keeps nonessential lights off during the day because electricity is expensive, and squinting is cheap.

"After a few years, he died of blood poisoning," she continues, recalling this strange John Howard Griffin character. But she's an unreliable narrator. I've already read up on the author and the myths around his death. "They think it was all the toxins he put into his body to turn his skin black."

"At first, I couldn't even guess what medication he used,"

I say, without contradicting her. I have a professional interest in how someone might become properly Black. "Turns out it's for vitiligo, that autoimmune disease where your body attacks your pigment cells and turns you white like Michael Jackson. And after that, he sat in front of a UV lamp for four days. And after that, he decided he still wasn't black enough, so he touched his face up with stain."

Specifically, the medication he used was called methoxsalen. The ethics of prescribing a dangerous drug for a journalistic vanity project are questionable; even his dermatologist admitted some reluctance. But John Howard Griffin didn't die from blood poisoning. The mundane truth is he had several heart attacks, then spent his last years in failing health. Eventually, he died from complications of diabetes. Fiction is stranger than truth.

"So, you read this book while you were a university student in Prince Edward Island," I summarize, "and you decided the white folks there were less racist than the ones in the United States."

"Oh, absolutely," replies my mother.

"They gave you a choice of any topic in the world, and you wrote them a term paper called *The Negro in America*."

"Yes."

"Then you moved to Toronto and married a British man."

The whitest of British men.

"Christopher, there weren't any Black people around back then!"

"But, in the end, you felt victimized by white people. All of them. That's…an emotional rollercoaster."

My fingers carelessly flip through the pages of *Black Like Me*. I sense the harshness of my spoken words, although I'm just trying to chip away the contradictions, perform an archaeological dig to clarify her true feelings about the white devil. I feel guilty giving her a hard time, so I laugh to break the tension.

"When I read it," I continue, redirecting my scepticism, "I don't get that ring of truth. Authenticity. You can tell when something is authentic. This guy refers over and over to this *hate stare*, this way white people would look at him in blackface as if they were disgusted."

"You don't think that's what he experienced?"

"How am I looking at you right now?" I say, unsure if my expression is as inscrutable as it feels.

"I don't know."

"Neither do I. Isn't that how people go through life? Their faces are inscrutable. Their motives are inscrutable. Their expressions are incidental, like their shoes or their hat. Who knows what's happening underneath?"

"I don't think it crossed *anybody's* mind to doubt his story. Christopher, put your shoes on."

"Even if he could remember all these conversations," I continue, "they couldn't be accurate transcriptions. His characters, they speak in complete paragraphs without interjections or pauses. The only person I know who speaks in complete paragraphs is *you*."

She laughs and makes for the front door, me in pursuit, lobbing another volley of complaints after her about this bizarre book.

"It's instinct. We just know when something is true. A good writer knows how to tell a fictional story and make it feel true. There's a rhythm and cadence to it."

"You've written books," says my mother. "Have you found that balance?"

"Who knows. Time will tell. Maybe it doesn't matter if something is completely true, so long as it makes a good story."

"Maybe, Christopher." She stops at the hall closet,

having obviously lost interest in the philosophical path this conversation has taken.

"The whole book comes across like a fever dream of Old Southern racism. My guess is the author was there, and that snippets of these events probably happened. But I don't believe all of it. Maybe it was *based* on a true story."

"Maybe, Christopher." She slips into the tattered blue jacket she uses for gardening. It used to be mine three decades ago, back when I was her size. "Put your shoes on and come outside. I have three chores for you."

I obediently follow her into the cold. She heads for the garage, where she produces two rakes, neither of which is much younger than the jacket.

Maybe seventy-seven years is the perfect time to ask somebody about the life they've lived. Whether she'll make a more reliable narrator than John Howard Griffin is hard to say. What she needs is a critical ear, an investigative journalist. Life has few absolute heroes or villains. But one thing sticks: that my mother is a more authentic vessel for the Black experience than a white man in blackface.

# 18. INDIGENOUS AFRICANS OF ST. LUCIA

Orange piles dot the lawn like termite mounds. Organized, already raked, soon to be bagged, even if new leaves will sprout again in the spring, then fall from the same trees next autumn. That's entropy, the way all things gravitate towards disorder, and it's a five-star word of the day. Life is about reversing it. Maybe there's more, but it's all built on a foundation of shirt-tucking, list-writing, bed-making, clothes-hanging, and lawn-raking.

Or maybe not. My friend Melody wants to be a tree when she dies, and have mushrooms grow around her remains.

*Death is death*, she said.

*That's a tautology*, I told her.

*What's a tautology?* she asked.

Tautology: the needless repetition of an idea, statement, or word. Word of the day.

My mother wields the good rake, leaving me with its battle-worn brother. Its rusted claws are wildly deformed and all-but useless. Conscripting me and these muddy gardening gloves to wage war on this lawn with this rake is a more Sisyphean task than any mushroom person would have the patience for, and besides, my mother is reluctant to surrender the slightest control of the operation. She pays better attention to the details of the work, aiming for golf course-calibre perfection. She's more organizer than mushroom person, and the evidence is everywhere, from towels to taxes to recipes to photo albums.

Photo albums, recipes, tax files and towels resist entropy, but still demand diligence: time and energy. Get it wrong and leave behind only wretched disorganization. A wealth of detail lost to posterity.

"Mom, what part of Africa did my great-grandmother come from?" I ask, transferring an armful of leaves into the temporary order of the leaf bag.

"She's not African," my mother corrects me. "She's Black from the West Indies, from St. Lucia. But she was one-quarter white. She used to work for a white family as their servant, and the landowners would have these rich meals every day. And she'd come home every night with all the exotic treats that were left over."

"But what about *before* St. Lucia?" I insist. "You've never talked about her."

It's unlikely my great-grandmother's ancestors were native to that tiny island, that the Spanish conquistadores stumbled upon a small band of migrant Africans when they made landfall in the New World. The indigenous Africans of St. Lucia. Maybe they sprouted from the Caribbean soil like mushrooms. But I can't accept at face value that this is where my family tree ends.

"She slept in my bed for half my life growing up," continues my mother. "The boys in one bed, two of them facing upward and one facing downward. The girls in another bed. And me, with our grandmother. She died next to me, right there in that bed."

An awkward morning indeed.

"Right," I say, distracted by the busywork of moving leaves from one arbitrary location to another. "But you never asked her where she came from? Whether she remembered arriving on a slave ship, in shackles and chains, singing freedom songs?"

"I don't know when she came to Trinidad from St. Lucia. Or why. Or how. Maybe she swam."

"And your grandfather? He didn't come with her?"

"I don't know, Christopher. We weren't curious. We weren't educated to ask questions about our heritage."

Neither was I, until today. Such questions seem important – to experience the horror of slavery and live to tell the tale is something powerful. But refugees are often reluctant to tell their stories. *Pushing for disclosure of traumatic events in well-functioning individuals may result in more harm than good.* That's what the medical establishment recommends, last I checked, and someone even published it in a journal. Paradoxically, those stories need telling the most, lest those powerful experiences fade into the indifference of the universe – the nuance, colour, joy, and pain of entire lives replaced by a single anecdote about a cramped bed.

That thought lingers as I lean into the leaf bag, shoving an armful of curled and brittle leaves to the bottom. My great grandmother's experiences are gone, presto, vanished from the plane of existence. What remains are wisps of memories trapped inside my mother's head – a smoky trail after a candle is extinguished, shades of mental images, a creaky bed, and whatever strands of DNA were passed down to her descendants. Genetics are the only memory that nature cares for, never the original experience that got us there. My great-grandmother's impact on the world exists neither in text, nor spoken word. That link to the past is broken forever.

Several years ago, backpacking in Ghana, I met a Black revolutionary scholar in a photography museum in Cape Coast. He had a wide face and cunning eyes, and the room around us was a dog's breakfast of dusty antique frames, black and white images, and stacked leatherbound books that smelled like an old trunk. *They want us to forget our history.* He meant the colonizers and slavers that brought Blacks across the ocean to the New World in a festering cargo hold, then broke their links to Mother Africa by assigning them all-new names. He said they could never have severed those ancestral links so completely without some help along the way, and he said so in a voice resonant enough to crush any doubt. It wasn't my fault, though. Why wouldn't he stop staring at me?

"You need to push the leaves down." My mother nudges me aside and leans in to force the leaves to the bottom "See? Fill all the space in the bag."

Organize. The dream of every narcissist and tyrant is to be a story important enough to be told, deluded by fantasies of infamy and immortality. But all stories are eventually forgotten. A thousand words for a picture, but fleeting moments of living are more priceless than a thousand pictures. In the end, most stories have been told already; they mimic the same archetypes, tension, heroism, oppression, sacrifice, cruelties, and conflicts of all human existence.

My mother has a story trapped inside her too, I'm certain of it. One that transcends her life, and these leaves.

# 19. CAVE DRAWINGS AND BLACK MAGIC

The two outstanding jobs involve loading winter tires into the trunk of the car, followed by wrestling an enormous patio umbrella from its stem and hauling it to the garage for seasonal hibernation.

As my mother bends to fasten a plastic tarp around the umbrella, I send Avani a screenshot of the letter Bell Canada rejected, and whose contents summarize my meagre knowledge of the court case. She's unimpressed.

"That won't get their attention," she texts as I follow my mother indoors. "It looks like you have a superficial understanding of what happened, and you're just expecting them to hand you money for your trouble. Big corporations aren't charities. They're smarter than that. Maybe if you dangled some negative media attention, but even then, they won't react unless they're under *threat*."

Another splash of cold water. My knowledge of my mother's life is a mishmash of disjointed anecdotes and trivia. On any visit to the suburbs, filling those gaps has never been urgent. But it feels urgent now.

"Hmmm," I text back.

"Well, ask her about it," suggests Avani, softening her tone. "Every parent has a secret life their kids are unaware of, right? I wish we had a time machine, so we could witness what they were like now that we're old enough to understand the complexities of the world."

I don't have the time machine, but I know my mother would reject the idea that she has a secret life. She claims to have no secrets, no skeletons among the towels, and I'm inclined to believe her. Now safely back inside in the house, I throw myself upon the regal armchair in the den and plunge in, demanding to know what kind of busybody ends up being a complainant in a Canadian Human Rights Tribunal.

"I don't know why you suddenly want to reminisce," she says, facing me from the opposite couch with her hands folded across her lap.

That's permission to press ahead.

"Start from the beginning, like you don't know me," I suggest, "and I'll stop you at the end. Start from right after your grandparents sprouted from the ground in St. Lucia."

She laughs. "But you *do* know me."

And I do know the basics: seven siblings, twenty-one years coming of age in Trinidad. Four girls born within a year of each other, three younger brothers. My grandmother lost three more children, one stillborn before my mother and two miscarriages in her eighth and ninth pregnancies.

"That wasn't unusual," she says. "That's just the way it was in our primitive Catholic communities."

"Wait." I lean forward on my throne to examine this morsel. "*Primitive?* What kind of word is that?"

"What else do you call superstition? We were middle class, but nobody knew how to stop babies from happening." She laughs and doubles down. "And we believed in obeah and black magic. So, primitive, yes."

Obeah is the brand of necromancy brought to the West

Indies by transplanted West Africans. Say the *Our Father* backwards and you can summon Satan, even though the devil is an unwelcome guest among the God-fearing, and even though in Trinidad, summoning him is punishable by six months in prison or a lashing. Rumour has it my aunt used instruments of obeah – whether blood, bone, or images – to murder my grandmother and steal her property. No one in the family has spoken to her since. Every good Roberts agrees on the above facts, although some revisionists might call obeah mere ancient spirituality, an ambiguous practice unfairly maligned and outlawed by colonial influences. Wait. Suddenly, I'm exhilarated to be here at the beginning.

I bang out another text to Avani.

"Avani, I'm doing what you said, and we're five minutes in. How would you feel if I called Zimbabwe *primitive*?"

"I'd be offended," she answers immediately. "*You* can't call it primitive."

The implication is that growing up there gives her the right to call Zimbabwe anything she chooses. And so too my mother, *vis a vis* Trinidad. A lengthy silence follows, in which I imagine her blood reaching a gentle boil. Then she adds:

"The word implies *unsophisticated*, but developing

countries are complex in the best and worst ways. They're just not on the same playing field as the West. Yet."

Her words are elegant and academic, and she's right. *Primitive* is blunt, insistent, and loaded with implications and raw emotion. It makes people feel and say things. It's one of our very best words.

# 20. MOSTLY PEACEFUL PROTESTERS

Trinidad is a melting pot, thanks to three hundred years of transatlantic slave trading that stretched into the 1800s and which was followed by waves of Indian and Chinese indentured servants, not to mention white European settlers. *Black* is a label that only means anything in opposition to being white. Its usefulness is blunted among people of innumerable shades of brown, and among variably pigmented Trinidadians, my mother grew up as a fish in water.

"But what about shadeism?" I ask her, referring to the pigment hierarchy among lighter-tinted folks of the same race.

"People say racism doesn't exist in Trinidad," she responds, shaking her head. "No, shade didn't make a difference. You could still get a job in the bank, or whatever it was you qualified for. We didn't grow up making people feel bad about their skin colour. Back then, I wasn't racially conscious yet. I only had positive experiences in Trinidad and even when I first arrived in Canada. I didn't run into real racism until I met Bell."

I retreat to the kitchen. I had expected my mother to admit that Trinidad is no Garden of Eden, that it's had its share of unrest over the years, just like anywhere else. That it turns out that wherever you go in the world, somebody is upset about race, imperialism, or both. I've saved an article on my phone for just this occasion. A summary of the Black Power Revolution that was active in Trinidad between 1968 and 1970, inspired by the Civil Rights movement in the United States. An article whose writer accused the supposedly independent Black government of aping the British, operating as a tool of imperialism – of being what he called *Afro-Saxons*.

Fighting words. In the spring of 1970, police murdered a protester named Basil Davis in the capital, Port of Spain, and it sparked general strikes, mass marches, and a State of Emergency. *After curfew*, reads another article, *anyone outside would be beaten, shot, robbed, raped, imprisoned, or all of these, by the police.* Thirty-five thousand mourners attended Basil's funeral.

I return to the living room and float this out to my mother.

"Do you remember the Black Power movement?" I ask. "When I read about it, it sounded a bit like the George Floyd thing."

She gives me a blank look.

"No, most of the family was outside the country by then. If it was 1970, I guess that must have been the year after I left Trinidad for the last time. And now, I'll never go back. I can't stand the heat, and all the roaming mongrel dogs. All I remember from back then is there was some tension between the Blacks and the Indians."

I fact-check this too. Sure enough, when an East Indian department store called Kirpalani's was torched during a Black Power protest, conservative Indians insisted that the Pan-Africanism movement had turned them into as much the enemy as whites. If history repeats itself, the spokespeople for Black Power might have countered by claiming their protests had been *mostly peaceful*.

"I think the Blacks didn't like the Indians," says my mother when I summarize the events. "Back then, the Indians weren't educated. They were poor too."

Her disarming bluntness makes me laugh. I'm not offended, because eighty years on this planet gives you licence to say anything you want about its inhabitants. Only Millennials tiptoe around unacceptable thoughts for fear of losing their livelihoods.

"So, you never came back to Trinidad during the Black Power movement?"

"It didn't affect me," she says. "By 1970, I was already married. And once I was in Canada, I stopped being interested in what was happening in Trinidad. Don't forget that after I left home, my family all started leaving right afterwards. My father left the very next year. Angela was the only one who came back because she couldn't stand the New York winters."

"That's the only reason?"

"She hated being cold."

"So, she came back to the wild dogs and constant heat?"

"Yes, Christopher," says my mother. "Can you blame her? I'm getting old enough to hate the thought of winter too."

I glance out the window at the sparsely populated branches of her maple tree, the deserted street, and the dense grey sky above. Fifty-five winters, to be exact, and another on the way.

## 21. BASIC GREEK PHONOLOGY

Back when she was a Peace Corps volunteer in the Dominican Republic, Avani told me her elementary students could barely recognize the letters of the alphabet, let alone find their names on a written list.

No surprise. Leisure in the tropics meant gossiping over too-sweet coffee, swaying hips to *bachata*, or hitting a baseball, not hiding in a corner with a book. Parents knew this even better than their children, for whom they set the example. Besides, what corner could anyone find? Maybe it was only a Dominican thing or maybe it was pan-Caribbean, but a childhood without books was foreign to me. Here, my bookshelf is packed with books whose complexity tracks my development, from the Berenstain Bears and Peter Rabbit, to Roald Dahl and the Hardy Boys, to Arthur C. Clarke and JRR Tolkien.

"My parents were strict," says my mother when I repeat Avani's anecdote. She tells me how she only socialized with three or four other families and wasn't even allowed to play in the street with the other neighbourhood children. They figured she had plenty of brothers and sisters to fight with if she was bored.

"My sisters always said I was different. I was the studious one winning all the academic awards and I never got in trouble. Not like Angela. She'd raid the neighbours' fruit trees. And I would curl up alone on the veranda, reading for hours. No one *bribed* me into reading. I taught myself because it was my passion. Trinidad is sixty miles long and forty miles wide but reading let me imagine a world no one I knew had ever experienced. I don't even understand how I got so obsessed. My parents weren't readers; Mum sewed clothes, and Daddy drove a cab."

I nod, but she's on a roll. She'll continue without my encouragement. And she does just that, telling me how her first memory of injustice somehow involved reading.

"They punished me when I was three years old for reading aloud to the older children."

"Wait, what toddler goes to school when they're three?" I ask, burying her lede. "And how could you possibly remember back that far?"

"I remember it like it was yesterday. We called her *Teacher Van*, and her schoolhouse was right down the block. The older kids knew full well I could read, and one day they wrote a four-letter word on the chalkboard and pretended they couldn't pronounce it. We never used that language at home, so when I sounded the word out, it could have been Greek. When Teacher Van arrived, they told her what I had said. And as punishment, I got a few smacks with the ruler."

"You came clean? Should have lied," I suggest. "Wasn't this before phone cameras and surveillance footage and Rodney King videos?"

"Christopher, I was three years old. I didn't know how to lie. I just knew something unfair was happening, and that's why I remember it so vividly. The punishment bothered me for a long time. When my mother found out, she went into the school the next day to plead my case."

I don't press, but experience has convinced me that three-year-olds make the best liars.

# 22. THE PROUD FATHER

Do Black folks value education?

Maybe it's the wrong question, and a silly one at that. First, we'd have to crack the word *Black* open like a piñata, lean over the resulting mess and inspect the contents. Even then, we'd be left with a shambles of unhelpful anecdotes, stereotypes, and generalizations.

Like the time I dated a Ghanaian girl. She was attractive and religious, like most Ghanaian girls, and she placed enormous pressure on herself to impress her demanding academic father who wielded an advanced degree in engineering. She already worked full time, but among friends, her true passion was her cosmetics ecommerce business and side hustle as a backup dancer. That was problematic: good West African families value few things more than a structured education and moral purity. Having a daughter who was a talented dancer would never do. And when she finally enrolled in graduate school, I could never tell whether she was genuinely interested in the material, or just needed to pile a few prestigious letters after her name.

When it comes to North Americans, I'm left picking through my own limited experiences. As far as Caribbean Blacks, I have only stories passed down by my mother. *Lived experiences*, some call them. If only a single, harmonious Black consciousness existed to speak for us with a single voice and resolve matters for good.

"Firstborns just mature faster," my mother continues, explaining how Caribbean Blacks value education. "Except when it came to social maturity, because of how overprotective my parents were. But all the expectations placed on me made me competitive. I hated Daddy, but he would give me prizes every time I topped the class in term examinations. Depending on how much money we had, it was anything from a wristwatch to a bicycle. Once, he bought me a new bookcase."

"Hated him? Sounds like he was proud of you."

A grunt. "We all hated him. Angela still has nightmares."

"Nightmares?"

"Well, his other family across town didn't help, for starters. He had to stretch his money to support his mistress and her children, so we never had enough. And he would hit us for misbehaving."

Corporal punishment doesn't sound off-brand for a mid-twentieth century pants-wearer in the Caribbean. I wonder how many 1950s fathers spared the rod – and how many Caribbean fathers led secret lives across town. Again, there's no surveillance footage to check.

"Isn't that exactly what you expected of a father back then?" I say, navigating a treacherous path. "A disciplinarian who loved you only conditionally, and who delivered corporal punishment predictably? And who rewarded you for making him proud?"

A long pause. Maybe I've won her over with my implication that 1950s dads were *supposed* to be abusive, even the rare times they came home sober.

"I don't think so. He never hugged and kissed us."

She's missing my point, so I try again. "Were ethnic fathers really known for affection back then? Nowadays, it's *white* parents who want to be your best friend. White parents want you to do what makes you happy. They want to support your dream of being a poet. They want to toss the football in the backyard and go fishing on the weekend. Ethnic parents want to teach you that life is hard, and the sooner you learn it, the better."

She shakes her head. I haven't won her over at all.

"I don't know, Christopher," she says. "But I had nothing to say to that man after I turned sixteen."

## 23. DEFENSE AGAINST THE DARK ARTS

"When I was twelve," she continues, "we had the island-wide entrance examinations. The biggest filter you ever saw."

Those examinations determined who would win scholarships and whose educations would end unceremoniously. My mother placed second in her school and fourth on the entire island, which opened her options considerably. Her score earned her a scholarship at St. Joseph's School while my brothers and sisters were placed in other schools.

St. Joseph's was a Roman Catholic convent founded in

the nineteenth century by the Sisters of St. Joseph, and the neighbouring all-girls school was the nuns' source of income. At the time, it was the highest regarded private school in Trinidad, but when they ran into some financial trouble, the government announced they would subsidize the Sisters if they made every third class a scholarship class. They began offering full tuition to the top twenty students in Trinidad every year, from Grade Seven onward.

The convent school was run by the nuns themselves and a few day teachers. Most of the paying students were wealthy boarders from Venezuela and Curaçao, and they lived in the garret of a three-storey wooden building across the lawn. The rest of the wealthy ones came other West Indian islands like St. Kitt's – often from families of former slaveowners – and they had grown up on plantations where they could look out over the other islands from their balconies. The Venezuelans were mostly in the regular academic stream, and they rarely mixed with the scholarship students. For the next six years, academic and athletic achievement were the keys to social acceptance.

"Everybody knew how the school was divided, how it was segregated, that the *A-stream* was the scholarship class where everybody knew *everything*!"

"Apartheid by intelligence," I add.

"They divided us again into four houses which competed in sports, conduct, and comportment: *Mary Immaculate Queen* in blue, *St. Joseph* in yellow, *Saint Maria Geretti* in red, and *Blessed Anne Marie* in green. I was voted dorm prefect, and Vice-Captain of my house in senior year."

"Sounds like you went to school at Hogwarts," I interject.

"What?"

"Four houses. Like Hogwarts School of Witchcraft and Wizardry. Or maybe, *St. Joseph's School of Obeah and Necromancy.*"

My *Harry Potter* reference goes unappreciated. Rather than amused, she's flustered that I won't let her continue.

"I don't know what Hogwarts is."

"You know, the four houses."

"No, I don't know."

"Forget it. Tell me more about apartheid at the convent."

"They posted the results of every examination on the classroom door, with all the students ranked from one to twenty." She opens her arms as if to embrace the room from the ceiling to the floor. "Everybody knew exactly who was on top, and who was at the bottom."

"That wouldn't do nowadays," I point out.

"Of course not," my mother admits. "But the scholarship stream loved the competition!"

"I wonder how much the person ranked twentieth loved the competition." I laugh.

"Can you imagine the shame? It was a different era. The convent was a fun place to be, but only if you were bright."

"Not to mention," she continues, "how the nuns nurtured our purity and innocence. They discouraged any socializing –"

"Like your parents."

"—and they inculcated obedience. They implored us to resist all temptations. There was an all-boys school across the street, run by fathers of the holy order. But our schools never interacted beyond the occasional boy who came to our attention because of his good looks or athletic prowess. Our virtue had convinced us that some reward awaited us – if not in this world, then certainly in the next one. Did you know that by graduation day, half my class was seriously considering the Church as a vocation? Mmm hmm. We wanted to become Sisters ourselves."

## 24. CHICKEN AND EGG

"What about your father?"

"I told you; I stopped talking to him when I was sixteen. And I'll tell you why. Do you remember that deep lot behind the house in Port of Spain, with all the fruit trees and vegetables?"

"No."

"It was huge. We had dogs and chickens and ducks roaming about. Every Sunday, Mum would run around that garden and catch a chicken to cook for dinner. I don't think I could ever do that. We grew up in that house, and none of us ever learned how to kill a chicken."

"You just break its neck," I say, as if this were no big deal, something I could do in a pinch. No wild suburban chickens out here to call my bluff.

"And sometimes," my mother continues, "she would kill it and it would hop around headless before it died. It was awful, but…" she brightens, "we always had wonderfully fresh eggs. I tell everyone about those eggs, but no one knows about them. Have I told you about the eggs?"

"Refresh my memory."

"Well, a chicken lays an egg every day. But when you kill the chicken and look inside, it has a whole string of eggs in different stages of development. You have the one ready to come out the next day, and that one has a soft shell. And then, the one after that has barely the *film* of a shell. And the next one has no shell at all. And eventually, you just see a yellow blob that gets smaller and smaller as you make your way down the string."

"And when you get to those naked eggs, they're *sweet*. Unbelievably delicious. I don't know what they do with those eggs when they kill chickens here. The only person I could talk to about any of that, the only one who even knew what I was talking about, was Leon in Prince Edward Island. He came from rural Massachusetts, and they had chickens there too."

That's a familiar name.

"Leon always comes up, doesn't he?"

My mother ignores this. She's fully immersed.

"Anyway, our family dog found out that our hen was laying an egg every single day. It started showing up early to steal the egg and eat it, until we couldn't get eggs from the hen anymore. To be honest, I don't even know where you would begin breaking that habit out of a dog.

"When Daddy found out, he was furious. One day, we had a family dog, and the next day when we came home, there was no dog. He had taken our dog and either killed it himself or put it in the dog pound. We never found out which one."

"Yikes."

"He never said anything to us. He just went and did… whatever it was he did with our dog. And all seven of us were confused and angry and hurt, so I spoke up for the family because I was the oldest.

"I challenged him. I looked at him across the room and said, *how could you do that?* And he walked straight up to me without a word of warning and struck me *pow!* Hard, across the face, so hard that he made my nose bleed. *You don't talk to your father like that!* And so, I didn't talk to my father like anything after that. I was sixteen and that was the last time I had anything to say to him. He never apologized, and I didn't speak to him again for my entire last five years in Trinidad."

# 25. THRESHOLD GUARDIAN

---

She continues.

"Graduation approached, and neither of my parents provided any advice on what would happen afterwards. We didn't have guidance counsellors or mentors to discuss careers or retirement goals. All I knew was that after high school, people went out and got *adult jobs*.

"All that mentoring is so essential nowadays – but back then, we led a simple life. People spent their whole life in the same community, ran into the same people year after year at church, Sunday walks, the beaches, and the neighbourhood stores and groceries. We knew when someone was born or died. We knew when someone's daughter or son got married. We knew the in-laws. Nobody *planned* their life. Nobody *planned* on children, abortions, or divorce. People just lived according to their moral code and the Golden Rule. And that's what I expected my life to become too."

If she's hoping to build suspense, my mere existence is proof enough this didn't happen.

"Until?"

"Until one day, the principal and school director cornered me a week before graduation. They asked me if I'd considered my future. When I said I hadn't, they offered me a job teaching at the convent school."

They expected her to cover subjects from Languages to Religion from grades eight through eleven. Having just finished the equivalent of grade thirteen, this was a tall order. It meant there would only be a two-year gap separating her from her upper year students. Nonetheless, she accepted and spent the next two years teaching at her former school.

"I enjoyed the challenge but became acutely aware of my own impossible standards. I was a Virgo, so I already expected perfection from myself. But those expectations now extended to my students too. I'd be disappointed in them if their grades fell below ninety percent. I was socially stagnant, and I worried that my inertia would deepen the longer I stayed at the convent. I'd turn into a prude, a shrew, and then an old maid.

"I dreamed of that world beyond Trinidad, where I could develop part of my character I was convinced existed. I settled on a drastic change: to leave home in the most respectable way, by going abroad to study. But I'd wait until I was twenty-one, when Daddy could put up no opposition."

"Why would he have put up any opposition?" I ask.

"He was a bully. And because I couldn't expect any help from my parents, I became a mercenary, saving as hard and as fast as I could. I left my prized teaching job for a more lucrative one at the Canadian Imperial Bank of Commerce in Port of Spain. No one gave me guidance on where to get a university degree either, no surprise there. So, I researched what I could, although in the end, my decision was based on rumours and speculation. I dismissed the American universities because I heard their standards were low and their education system was *bad*."

Her sweeping dismissal of the entire spectrum of American colleges seems overly broad, like claiming wild mushrooms are too poisonous, Indian food is too spicy, or politicians are too dishonest. Avoiding the United States strikes me as a rational decision, but for completely different reasons.

"Didn't it have more to do with civil rights movement?" I ask. "You could have accidentally enrolled in the University in Alabama, and then found your professors blocking the auditorium door and shouting, '*segregation now, segregation tomorrow, segregation forever'*."

"That happened?"

"That happened. Wasn't that part of your calculation?"

I continue: Wasn't Clennon King part of that calculation, a man committed to an asylum in 1958 for attempting to attend the University of Mississippi during an era of segregation that didn't fully end until a decade later? Klan crosses being burnt on the steps of law schools, professors cowed into silence over the controversy on whether classes should be separated like laundry. Choose the wrong school, and you've suddenly become a reluctant trailblazer, which sounds unpleasant, at the very least. But my mother wags her head back and forth.

No.

"People in Trinidad weren't obsessed with all this apartheid business. We lived in peace and harmony." Her voice becomes animated. "But we *did* talk about how England was racist, cold, and aloof. Everybody knew. Isn't that awful? We had two vastly different perspectives on England and America."

"Then why Canada?"

"Finances. Process of elimination. I wrote the Canadian Embassy for a list of universities, and then applied to St. Dunstan's, a tiny Catholic university in the smallest province,

Prince Edward Island. My upbringing meant I was keen to stay in an all-female residence called Marion College, which was occupied by Sisters. And despite all my hard work, I only had enough money saved for two years tuition and board, so I prayed for summer jobs that would take care of the rest. Then, two weeks before I left, Daddy approached me and offered to pay my airfare."

"Your *father*?" I say, incredulous. "Why the change of heart? Why would he suddenly cover your ticket?"

"I think he saw how determined I was. That now that I was an adult, he had no more control over my life. I had applied, I had been accepted, and I was clearly pleased with myself. I was going and he knew it. So, he resigned himself to it."

I reframe this in the language of the classic heroic journey. "He was a *threshold guardian* between you and a new world of adventure."

My mother ignores this.

"I wasn't looking for money, but I still said thank you and took his one-way fare. And then, in September 1964, off I went, bright eyed and innocent, never even having been on a real date. I arrived at the airport in Dorval completely alone, without a single friend or relative to greet me."

# PART TWO

# 26. MISCEGENATION AND OTHER PERVERSIONS

"In those days, what was the word?" I say, taking the reins. "I used to know it, before they outlawed it at the end of the seventies. Dating somebody of a different race. People don't say that word anymore."

"Miscegenation," says Christopher. He's lying on the living room floor like a child, with me on the sofa. "Word of the day. It means *interbreeding of different people considered to be different racial types.*"

"Why don't they use that word anymore?"

"Because it's offensive, mom! It makes interracial dating sound like…a reaction you'd come across in an organic chemistry textbook. Or some sort of perversion."

"Yes, that's what they thought," I agree right away, "and it was a serious offense in those days. Canada never enforced any laws, but in the United States, it was like apartheid in South Africa. They'd throw you in jail for miscegenation. Come to think of it, they'd throw *both* people in jail. And that's when I thought, *okay, now Leon knows he's in trouble*, because I was under the impression Massachusetts still had that law on the books."

"Wait, back up," says Christopher. "Leon again?"

Leon comes up a lot, I'd say.

"Back then," I continue, "miscegenation was still a felony in sixteen states, and Utah wouldn't even allow a marriage between a Negro and an octoroon. One-eighth Black blood was too much! As it turned out, Massachusetts law in the sixties would recognize an interracial marriage if the wedding were legal in one's home state. But how would anybody except a lawyer know that? Would you bring your papers with you? And the Supreme Court took until 1967 to finally outlaw all miscegenation laws as unconstitutional."

"That's all so foreign now," says Christopher. "Nowadays everybody wants beige, aesthetically ambiguous babies like me."

Is that right? Bigger question, is Christopher writing a book about me, or maybe one about Trinidad? Too many questions about subjects that never interested him before. All too suspicious but I'll indulge him because I have no secrets. Fine with me if he wants me to explain how a telephone company woke me up to the very real racism in Canada, and how it broke my childhood naivete. Somebody should hear it, even if they make me shout it from the rooftops. And if Christopher wants to take over my Bell Canada case, he's welcome to all of it.

"I'm open and honest. I have nothing to hide in my life," I say. "You're much more secretive than me. You never just spill your guts like I do."

"I don't see the use."

"Of what?"

"Of spilling my guts."

## 27. FASHIONABLE BOOTS AND OTHER TRIVIALITIES

"I don't know why you don't sit in a chair like an adult," I scold from the high ground.

"I'm fine like this."

Christopher rolls from his stomach onto his back, so I can see his face. Good enough.

"Over the years, there were anywhere from seven to nine foreign students – me from Trinidad, Angela Mohale from Lesotho. Doris, my roommate for the next three years, was one of the Hong Kong immigrants. All we had in common was none of us had ever seen snow. That first harsh Canadian winter was a shock to everyone."

"You've been to Prince Edward Island," I begin. He took me back for my birthday four years ago to explore the Charlottetown campus and the legacy of Anne of Green Gables. "But that was in August. The cold weather there begins promptly in September, and the blizzards follow by mid-October. Nothing melts until early May, and in between, the university would cancel classes for the worst of the snowstorms."

"When the locals passed by and told us what a lovely day it was, we raised our eyebrows they just couldn't be serious. But then we learned to appreciate it – the shivers, the cycle of digging our boots deep into the snow, struggling to extricate them, and then plunging them back in, all the way across campus. My new cardigan was hopeless against that cold."

"Yes, of course," Christopher says, brushing the carpet threads up and down. "Bone-rattling cold. But when do you get to the boyfriends?"

"Just wait." I won't deprive him of a single detail. "I lived in the convent with the nuns, and we would all file out to chapel at the crack of dawn for daily mass. The nuns lived on one end of our building, and the foreign students lived on the other. They assigned one nun to mother us, to tuck us into bed, and to make sure we weren't playing hooky. You'd only enroll there if you were *Catholic*, and I don't think any of us dreamed of skipping mass. We were good, nice, *innocent* children! Those nuns brought us up well. I always regret that I'm not around nuns anymore."

"With winter approaching, the nuns appointed local students to help us shop downtown for our new wardrobe. We should have come back with flat-footed sheepskin boots like the ones I wear now – but somehow, we came back with fashionable *heeled* boots that turned the icy walkways into a daily adventure. The boys were delighted whenever one of us crashed to the ground. *Nothing like this stuff in Trinidad, eh?* they would say to us."

"Seems a little ignorant unless you were walking with them," Christopher says, frowning. "And if they *were* walking with you, they should probably have helped you up."

"It was fun!" I exclaim. "We didn't mind falling! We were kids, eighteen, maybe nineteen years old. What did we care if we fell? And the boys just stood there watching, waiting for the foreign students to entertain them."

"I still think they were assholes."

"It was flirting! And then we'd hurry on towards the next classroom until one of us fell again."

## 28. ANOTHER DIGRESSION

"The island was like home," I continue. "I was happier than I had ever been in Trinidad. The islanders were down-to-earth rural folk who were genuinely curious about my background and family, and they welcomed me with open arms."

"When they invited us foreign students to their homes or to meals out on the town, it was a welcome change from the university cafeteria. One of the teaching priests, Father Larry Landrigan, was especially kind. He would take us for ice cream on Sunday afternoons at the local Dairy Queen, and sometimes he would even drive us to his house for home-cooked meals. In the winter, we would chat around a roaring fire. That was another new experience, because there wasn't much use for a roaring fire *indoors* in Trinidad or Africa. Father Larry was the one who really taught us about being Canadian. God Bless his soul."

"It must have seemed strange to set fire to your house on purpose," Christopher agrees. "But back up: didn't you call the people in Trinidad *primitive*? But the islanders were *down-to-earth*. What's with the double-standard?"

"I guess because we considered Canada more…"

Christopher lifts his head in anticipation. More interest than he showed in my fashionable boots. Had I called Trinidad *primitive*?

"Wait." It's a trap. "Why are you so critical of the word *primitive*? That's just what we thought back then."

"It's your own country! People get defensive about their roots."

"No," I say. "Come on. Immigrants from Third World countries know their countries are poor. Everyone in the West Indies would agree with that."

"Maybe," says Christopher, dropping his head back down. "But *down-to-earth* is more flattering than *primitive*. I think the right comparison would be if you described the islanders as hillbillies. Rednecks. I mean, I can see how someone who grew up in Prince Edward Island has every right to reclaim the word. But if an outsider called them hillbillies, they'd be rightly offended."

"Maybe, Christopher."

I'm bored with this game. What does it matter what word I choose? I dive back in, praying for fewer interruptions.

"Traveling between Father Larry's home and our residence sometimes meant navigating the unpredictable winter storms. We we'd be petrified and fascinated by the scarce visibility, the blur of dim headlights emerging from nowhere, the wet snow clinging to the windshield, and the wheels sliding helplessly as we turned corners. I didn't fully understand just how dangerous this drive was until my sophomore year, when a friend invited me to her home in the country for March break. Her brother offered to teach me to drive, and without warning me about ice, he set me loose on an isolated single-lane highway. He was in the passenger seat and my friend was in the back."

"I braked on a whim, and the car spun out of control. I gripped the steering wheel in horror and my passengers panicked in silence around me. The car skated across the black ice, and we narrowly missed a roadside mailbox before ending up in a ditch. We abandoned the vehicle to the snow drifts and walked back to the house to plan its rescue. It took me weeks to overcome the anxiety and nausea when I thought about it, and I didn't take the wheel again for seven and a half years."

Christopher is laughing, and I don't know why.

"But unless you end up dating Father Larry," he says, "we're on another tangent here. You're supposed to be telling me about university boyfriends and white devils. Mom, this is why your stories take *so long*."

## 29. TWO BLUE EYES

"Okay, but I'm just laying the foundation. That's how the island was in the sixties. Simple, innocent, down-to-earth. One Christmas, a woman wanted someone to babysit her two toddlers, two and four years old, and I took the job. I found out the kids didn't understand *why* I was this colour.

They asked me if I ate too much chocolate ice cream."

Christopher smiles.

"Did you and Angela ever feel self-conscious being the only two Black people at the school – like someone had appointed you to represent the entire race?" he asks. "I bet most of the islanders had never even seen a Black face before. Or maybe they had on the news, or in books. Maybe they'd heard rumors you arrived on boats wearing loincloths and carrying spears."

"Not really," I say, simply. "All the foreign students had plenty in common, no matter what colour. For one, we were all serious, hardworking, and determined, especially the Chinese ones. Me, I was motivated by the fear of failure, and the dread of being sent home with my tail between my legs. I couldn't predict how Canada's standards would compare with Trinidad, and the stakes were high because I was paying my own way through school."

"At first, I plunged into my studies with the same intensity and dedication as in Trinidad, and both my roommate Doris and I were pleased with our first semester grades. That only motivated us more. We challenged each other to top the freshman year. She placed second in our university class, but

I still won our competition. I averaged over ninety percent and won a scholarship and some individual course prizes. They put my photograph in the Charlottetown newspaper, and they even sent the press release onward to Trinidad."

"Wow," says Christopher. "What did your parents say to that? What did your father say?"

I ignore him. They must have been proud, but nothing my father could have said would have mattered in the slightest.

"But predictably," I continue, "all this co-education had a creeping effect, and my social instincts gradually awakened. No surprise my first date was a boy from an island family of fifteen that had several priests and nuns. Even my date himself was a St. Dunstan's grad who had recently left the priesthood for the lay life. He was decent and easygoing, and he had a dry sense of humor. We saw each other a few times over the next three years."

"Eric." His name lands in my consciousness like a rolled-up newspaper on a doorstep. If I have no romantic interest in a man, I never notice the eyes, but his are etched in my memory forever. "Piercing blue eyes. He took me home to meet his parents on my first Christmas in Canada. And I thought, Jesus Lord, what am I getting myself into? And sure enough, that boy stuck to my side *like glue*."

"The other foreign students resented socializing with white students, but not me. I was outgoing, and I'd help anyone, academically or otherwise. For the most part, I treated both males and females equally, but now I noticed that boys provided a different perspective on life than my girlfriends. And suddenly, it was easy to be well-liked by the boys."

"Wait," says Christopher. "Angela Mohale and the Chinese students wouldn't socialize with the white students? But that only leaves the male foreign students."

"What male foreign students?" To be honest, I never saw another Black person on Prince Edward Island after Angela Mohale. "Angela came from Lesotho. You should look it up on a map. The whole country was encircled by apartheid South Africa. She wouldn't talk to anybody who was white – not *one single person*. That's how she was brought up. She never went out because she just wasn't comfortable talking to white guys."

"But you were?"

"Of course! They were human beings! And back then, I barely knew what apartheid was, let alone what it meant."

"Strange not to have any Black international students."

I shrug. "Prince Edward Island is a thousand miles from anywhere. Probably the only reason I ended up there was I insisted on a Catholic school with nuns."

"Mom, the white boys."

"Yeah," I continue. "By second year, I realized I'd underestimated my popularity. Rumor had it the junior class wanted me as their candidate for Winter Carnival Queen. I had never considered myself beautiful, so I was flabbergasted when they chose me over a blonde beauty I would never have dreamed of beating. Then again, it wouldn't be the first time they chose a pageant winner based on intelligence, popularity, and congeniality."

Christopher interrupts again. "Crazy to have a Black Carnival Queen in 1960s Prince Edward Island, of all places. Kind of disorienting. Last thing you'd expect, like having a white face show up at the roti counter."

"Unexpected, maybe," I agree. "But either way, the final judges came from outside the university, and they didn't end up giving me the campus title. I was honored just to be nominated. It was my first and only television appearance – a local talk show – and my picture was in the newspaper again. And maybe because beauty queens are always the targets of university athletes, my dates after that were always hockey, basketball, and football players. I loved the attention, all the Valentine's cards and Christmas cards. I even got some anonymous cards from secret admirers when our hockey team won their away games. I remember running away just to avoid the boys I didn't want to have to turn down. And my friend Leo was my guardian angel back then. He'd protect me until the one I wanted finally asked me out."

"Doesn't sound like much stigma around interracial dating," Christopher concludes. "You didn't sense any anger from the locals when you were out on the town with a white boyfriend on your arm? Maybe I'm wrong, but Prince Edward Island just doesn't sound that racist."

"Of course, it wasn't!" The implication horrifies me. "Why would anyone be angry? It was an *honour* for the boys to take me out. This was a *little country place* where everybody accepted everybody."

# 30. ONE GREEN EYE, ONE BLUE EYE

"Let me continue, Christopher. When you're my age, you'll find you reflect more and more on the years gone by."

"I already told you my social life was taking on more importance. I still studied, but without my usual fanatical zeal. It turned out average work habits were sufficient for most classes. So instead, I gave myself space to develop the part of me I'd starved in Trinidad. As graduation approached, I concentrated on my French thesis. That meant I spoke as much French as I could with my boyfriend, Ron Turner, who was a popular student from Montreal--"

"--two birds, one stone."

"Sure. He planned on postgraduate studies in law after leaving the island. We were inseparable. By then, we'd been going steady for three months and spent almost all our time together, despite Angela Mohale warning me not to get hurt. I was naïve because I'd never been hurt that way before. Hurt meant physical pain, like stubbing a toe, and I thought she meant protecting myself morally as a good Catholic. So, I was confused and unprepared when he left at Christmastime to spend his holidays in Montreal without even bothering to say goodbye. When he returned to campus in January, he avoided me completely. No explanation."

"Nowadays, we have a word for cutting somebody off like that," says Christopher. "Ghosting."

"That's exactly it," I say. "And to complicate matters, I began dating other people shortly afterwards, including his roommate Mike, an American who had always been a close friend of mine. And later, I met Leon, a basketball player who had one blue eye and one green eye, and--"

"Wait, hang on," says Christopher, suddenly upright on the floor, animated. "His *roommate*? You went out with his roommate to get back at Ron? That's the most scandalous thing I've heard so far."

"Scandalous how? We'd already split up, and for an entire month, he didn't bother to tell me why. Mike and I, we'd just go out to dances and movies. Nothing scandalous about it. And then there was Leon, with that one blue eye and one green eye. Can you imagine?"

"Mom, you're burying the lede here. You're telling me about Leon's *eyes*, and I'm asking how you ended up dating your ex-boyfriend's *roommate*."

"Come on, Christopher. Besides, Leon even went to Ron beforehand to ask him if he could date me. Leon only told me about that much later. He didn't tell me until after Ron died."

The living room is grey, the only subdued light coming from the enormous window that looks across the front garden. Certain times in the summer, that sunlight can be blinding, but this late in the fall, daytime retreats by mid-afternoon. I pause, not sure how to approach the hardest part of this story, even though it happened ages ago.

"It was Easter break that shattered me. Ron must have been on his way to Montreal. Either way, that nun came to my room in the morning to say Ron had been in an accident. You can read it on someone's face, before they even speak, when you just don't know who's dead yet. Ron's cousin was driving. Two friends in the back. *Bam.* Head-on with a family of three in the other car. And out of that whole wreck, Ron was the only one still alive."

I pause again. Christopher nods, transfixed. He sits, rigid with his legs crossed and hands in his lap.

"Come upstairs," I say. "I'm going to show you something."

I stand and leave the living room with Christopher

trotting behind me, then weave my way up the spiral staircase. I crouch at the hall closet, momentarily shuffling through stacks of labelled documents before my fingers grasp a thin envelope. My whole life is in these reassuring piles, but this envelope is everything. I haven't touched it in years, but now is the right time to exhume it, since I can't shake the feeling that Christopher is penning my life story.

"When Ron got into that accident," I continue, opening the envelope and producing two pages of foolscap, "he was the only one who survived the night. Seven people. All the others died on the spot. The authorities called the convent to tell them what happened, and that nun said a prayer with us. Took us all down to the chapel. We prayed and prayed for him overnight, and then the next morning they told us he died too. He was alive Friday, dead Saturday. But I guess it was inevitable, because if he lived, he would have been a complete vegetable."

"Ron's best friend came from Montreal, and he and Mike cleared his things from his room in Prince Edward Island to take back home to the funeral. That day, they brought me a letter Ron had written the night before he left university for the last time. He had left it unfolded on his desk, almost like he expected it to be found. Look: it's two full pages long. Ron's friends said he'd been up writing it until one o'clock in the morning. They read it, and they decided it was something I should have. I think I've read it about a hundred times over the years. I used to read it and read it and read it when I was younger, and when the original got tattered, I made a photocopy. I still read it now and again."

I unfold the original and glance at it before passing it to Christopher. The paper is yellowed at the edges, oxidized, but in otherwise good condition, despite its brittle joints where I've lovingly folded it. Flawless cursive, parallel lines on the unruled foolscap, no strikethroughs. How could anybody's mind be so impeccably organized?

Christopher squints, eyes scanning the words. It's like part of Ron's soul is preserved in his artifact, not just because this letter exists, but because it's being read, fifty-three years after his death.

"I keep the original with his picture." I point to the black and white photo clipped to the letter. "Isn't he handsome in his glasses? Sit down and read it. I can't trust you with that away from my hands."

He obediently sits, cross-legged on the landing.

"In the letter," I continue, "he told me he knew I was

happy with Leon. He apologized and pledged his undying love, and his conviction that he would never find anyone else who compared. He explained why he ended our relationship, that he hated himself for being affected by me being Black, and him white. *Society imposed certain expectations*, he said. He couldn't have everything he wanted in a future with me, so he had to hurt me in a way he detested, since he knew racism would be something alien to my nature."

Christopher finishes reading and looks up.

"It puts most love letters to shame." He hands the letter back to me. "Guys don't write stuff like this anymore. I don't know if many women under forty have handwritten love letters these days. Maybe they should. I think it's nice."

"He has quite a flair for writing, no?"

"I'm impressed."

"You've never written a letter like that to anyone?"

"*No one* writes letters like that to anyone anymore. Most people wouldn't even know how to do it right. We only know how to send emails."

"You mean nobody knows how to expose themselves." I pause. "Do you think it sounds like a suicide letter? Look at that first line. *I don't usually write post-mortems.*"

"A little chilling," Christopher agrees. "But no, not taken by itself, not without some other context. Wait…you think he grabbed the steering wheel and yanked the car into oncoming traffic?"

I shrug, and then return the letter to its proper resting place inside the closet.

"I told a couple professors about the letter. One was a sociology professor who said he had questions too about a term paper Ron wrote. Who knows what was going through Ron's mind when he sat down to write that. But he was right about how it would affect me. I was devastated. Until then, I always assumed race didn't matter in the slightest. And now, someone I deeply cared for had died, and those memories of him were poisoned by this. I'd ruminate about it: why should someone's colour, religion or culture affect a relationship? I wondered if Ron ever would have been brave enough to give me that letter when he came back from Montreal, even just to relieve my nagging doubts that I'd done something wrong. I read the letter to the other international students, and they couldn't believe it. Later, I even told Father Larry the letter existed, although I couldn't bring myself to show it to him or say what was in it. Eventually, I got shy about showing it around."

I pause again.

"You act like it's rhetorical," Christopher says carefully, "but maybe it isn't. Maybe colour, and race, and religion have *everything* to do with a relationship. Especially back in those days – the stares, the stigma from friends and family and strangers in a place like Montreal. I don't really know how to put myself in the shoes of someone who's decided they should be with someone more…racially appropriate. All I know is it's not like that now, not here."

I bristle at the words *racially appropriate*, and then add one more thing.

"Left to my devices, I was too poor to even consider flying to Ron's funeral. But my closest friends held a private collection for my airfare. They put a ticket in my hand, and a few days later I left for Montreal. Everything from there is a blur. I can't even remember where I stayed. All I know is Ron's friends looked after me completely."

"His sister and parents told me I never left his coffin and didn't speak to anyone at the viewing. They said it looked like I had something private to say to Ron that I didn't dare say out loud."

They were right.

# 31. THREE REASONS WHY

"When I came back, I showed Leon the letter from Ron," I continue. "Looking back, maybe that was the same situation he eventually found himself in – not being able to accept I was Black – and now that he'd seen it, he couldn't very well turn around and tell me the same story. We dated a little longer, and then our relationship ended just like that, my head in a fog. Leon never told me why we broke up either. I was already in Toronto because I was two years ahead of him when I graduated, and when the time came for his graduation, he never even sent me an invitation. Later, I found out he got married to a *white* girl, a blonde girl from the island. I was heartbroken all over again. I didn't know why he did what he did, and I obsessed over all kinds of reasons why. And I still never believed it could have been *race* again. Can you imagine how innocent I still was?"

"What reasons did you come up with?"

"I had three reasons in my mind. First, remember I told you how he was an American from Massachusetts. His twin brother had been drafted into Vietnam, but he refused to go. He didn't have a valid exemption, so he went on the lam and hid somewhere. And as for Leon, he was exempted because he was studying at university. I decided that when Leon graduated, he was worried the army would draft him too, because the war was still in full swing. And his only way out was to stay in Canada and become Canadian – and I was no use to him because I was still fully Trinidadian."

"That would be a calculating move," says Christopher. "But what was the second reason?"

"Maybe he'd been fooling around with that blonde girl the whole time. Maybe he'd been doing something he shouldn't have been doing, and she *trapped* him. Maybe she lied and said she was pregnant, and he did the right thing and married her. He was a decent guy. But people used to play games like that because it was a disgrace to be pregnant and unmarried. Christopher, he married her *right away*, October of the year he graduated. The last time we exchanged letters was in March."

Christopher jumps on this with surprising gusto.

"Wait, you were in a long-distance relationship for *two years*? Pen pals. If you were apart from each other that long, wouldn't that reason be *number one?*"

I shake my head at this absurdity. Leon and I were more than just friends, and I know this full well having experienced it. "And kept up our writing to that degree? No. He even came to visit me once in Toronto. We spoke after he was married, and it felt just like it was yesterday."

"Okay." That's a dubious shrug, if I ever saw one, so I try to convince him one more time.

"Christopher, we didn't know the meaning of long-distance in those days. We wrote. Stamps were *five cents*."

"Mmmhmm." Christopher smiles. "A gumball at the soda shop was a penny and you could ride the trolley for a nickel. Okay, so you thought he took up with this white girl while you were back in Toronto. A decent guy doesn't do that. But let me guess, the third reason is racism. I just don't get why you'd rather believe he was *cheating on you*, than believe he was pressured by *societal expectations* the same way as Ron."

But I didn't have much choice what to believe.

"Fine," I say. "My third reason *was* racism. Maybe his mother got wind of who he was taking to graduation, and he realized his whole family would have to meet me. Maybe he was afraid to introduce me to his parents, because then it would be impossible to pretend that we weren't serious. And then it hit me he had already *seen* the letter from Ron, and how it affected me. He wouldn't dare send me another letter like that, knowing I'd been through it already."

"You're missing the point," Christopher interrupts. "How is it better for your mental health to believe it was racism, and not one of the first two reasons? Why assume anyone is racist without ironclad evidence? It's mind-reading. Paranoia. Aren't there enough reasons for people to be unpleasant to each other without adding one more?"

I don't know how to answer this, but the more television I watch – the more of these Black Lives Matter rallies I see on the news – the more hopelessly poisoned the world looks. "You have more experience with racism than me, because you're growing up amid all this hype."

"More?" says Christopher. "Come on, mom. Things are better every day. Nowadays, everyone my age wants to marry someone exotic, whether their parents like it or not. They want to travel the world, and love countries they don't belong to. I don't envy the old-fashioned white racists these days. The world rejects them. My generation casts the deplorables out into the fire."

# 32. GRADUATION DAY

"So how does this story end?" Christopher follows me back down to the den, then throws himself backwards onto the white carpet, as if making a snow angel.

"For the next few weeks," I answer, "I concentrated on finishing my thesis and preparing for final exams. I was the only one in my class doing a French major, and it took me a long time writing the paper. It turned out to be thirty typewritten pages, all in French, with all the little accents *aigu* and *grave* added in by hand. I was shocked the professor even asked me for a thesis, because they didn't ask anybody else for one to complete their majors. Maybe he was racist too."

"Really?" Christopher raises his head and a quizzical eyebrow, the look of amusement where he waits for me to admit I'm being flippant. But I won't climb down so easily.

"Looking back, I see a lot of racism I didn't recognize." Maybe everyone was out to make things just a little more difficult than necessary. Like riding on deflated bicycle tires. Either way, the emotional load of the past two years took its toll, and I was nowhere near as focused. I still graduated *cum laude*, but my grades were far from those of my freshman year. Even though only two students in my class had done better, graduating *magna cum laude*.

"Ron's parents wrote to me after the funeral. They came to visit on graduation day – that's somewhere around 1968 – and they congratulated me on my hard work and grades despite the tragedy. I couldn't bring myself to share their son's letter with them. But even after the ceremony, we kept in touch with regular letters and phone calls. They even invited me to his older sister's wedding in Montreal and came to visit me years later when I was already in Toronto. Just wonderful Canadians. Their family made me feel like I belonged, especially because we'd shared a common loss of someone we loved.

"But deep down, I couldn't forget their son had been capable of acting on attitudes that made me question whether I deserved the same happiness as my white counterparts. And I hated feeling like I had less worth because of my skin colour."

"So, in the end," asks Christopher, "was his family racist? They were the ones who raised their son to make the decisions he did."

"No," I answer without hesitation. "I don't know where

Ron got it from, because when I went to that funeral, his parents treated me like gold. They came all the way to Prince Edward Island to be with me for graduation because they knew I had no other family in Canada. They gave me that beautiful graduation photo of Ron, the one I showed you. And Ron himself, in his letter, he said he was the envy of everyone on campus when he saw how people reacted to seeing the two of us together."

# 33. ABAGBE ADEBAYO

Once my son sinks his teeth in, he's like a pit bull, jaws locked. Like now. Trying to tell me racism no longer exists in the workplace, not the same way it did – that old-fashioned racism is obsolete, like my own life experience makes me a stubby-armed dinosaur.

As usual, his rebuttal involves reading from his phone screen. His skepticism is perverse, and the more of it I hear, the less convinced I am that he will ever take on my Bell case.

"Sometimes racism needs to be *believed* to be seen," he

says, scrolling with gusto. When I decipher this riddle, I'm annoyed. Racism just needs to be seen to be believed, and you just need your two eyes. When it's in your face, what else could it be?

By now, the sun hangs low, dull light slouching through the bay window. The lights are off, and the den carpet is shaded with long shadows. Christopher is still on the floor.

"Here it is." He's still scrolling. "Mike says: *Wait until I send you guys the email I just got from work, with our new racial quotas. It says we need Black and Latinx managers to increase by fifty percent. I've gotta get out of this place.*"

"He has to quit his job," I clarify, "because they want to hire more minorities?"

My son laughs. I don't get it. Mike is thoroughly white, so why would he want to feather the nest of anyone except fellow white people? Maybe Christopher sees it differently, considering how he relishes tormenting me with his contrarian ideas.

"That's how it is everywhere now," he says. "Mike could protest that they should hire on merit instead of race, but he'd be swimming upstream, fighting on the wrong side of history. The only possible outcome is to drag his reputation through the dirt, maybe risk losing his livelihood. Anti-racism has allies, a whole social movement behind it. Tell me, who was this passionate about increasing Black representation back in the sixties?"

"Nobody," I admit. "That's not how it was."

"Take med school admissions," says Christopher. "Ten years ago, there were only three other Black students in my class of two hundred. We had two rows at the front of our lecture hall that everyone called the Great Wall of China and the Wailing Wall. Having only three Black medical students is *news*. No med school wants to be featured in the *Toronto Star*, and nobody wants another flood of Chinese, Indian, and Jewish grads. The applications are blind to race, but if you show up to the interview in black skin, you're already three steps ahead of the competition. Every corporation is starving for Black skin, and they don't care if it's attached to the Kenyan engineer who arrived on a commercial flight three hundred days ago or someone whose ancestors arrived in chains three hundred years ago. They don't care whether you're already part of the elite, or whether you're coming from a centuries-old underclass and low expectations. They just want pigment to brighten up the brochure."

I listen intently. He rarely tells me what he's thinking. Sometimes I think I do all the talking.

"There's another Black doctor who works at my hospital," Christopher says before I can get a word in. "She's Ghanaian and her name is Abagbe Adebayo. Just listen to *how awesomely Black* her name sounds. Imagine how Black somebody must be just to have that name. Now imagine somebody even Blacker, and *now* you have Abagbe Adebayo. She used to work in an A&E department in Manchester, England before she immigrated last year. And Abagbe Adebayo said to me one day, with her big West African accent, *What is everybody talking about here with this 'systemic racism?* She said nobody can even properly define it for her.'

That wasn't my experience. How could things be different now? For him to say discrimination vanished in a generation beggars belief. More likely racism just transforms. Hides in plain sight.

# 34. THERE AND BACK AGAIN

"Sit down in a chair. You're an adult, so start acting like one."

Christopher picks himself up and slides into the antique chair opposite me, fidgeting less than usual. I continue my story. I want to convince him that the promise of North America proved different from reality and convey that if the world were as idyllic as he claims, I would have already hammered out a settlement with Bell Canada.

"So, armed with my French degree," I continue, "I moved from Prince Edward Island to downtown Toronto. I'd always found Toronto fascinating because everything in Trinidad was one storey, maybe two. And when they called me to interview on the forty-second floor of a skyscraper downtown, I looked up at it from the street and panicked. *No way*. I was so terrified of that elevator that I took steps to avoid it, all forty-two flights of them. I had to rest a long time before my job interview just to catch my breath, and I knew I could never do that again. And that's how I got over my fear.

"Back then, not many people had an undergraduate

degree, and you'd be overqualified for most jobs if you'd even graduated high school. I felt ready for anything, and I first accepted a short-lived translation job handling Quebec correspondence for Simpsons-Sears before leaving for a better paid job in accounting at Gulf Canada. But then, my negligence caught up with me.

"I'd been lax about my visa. Everyone on Prince Edward Island had accepted that university students needed summer jobs, and our employers never bothered asking for work permits. By the time I had to swap my student visa for a landed immigrant, I learned those expiry dates were serious. They told me I couldn't apply within the country and sent me back to Trinidad while they processed my paperwork."

"My mom, the illegal alien." Christopher's interjection momentarily throws off my rhythm.

"Imagine being plucked and dropped back into Trinidad," I continue. "I was a stranger in my homeland. My old friends had new interests, and my accent had changed. I had to adapt to the lethargy of the Caribbean, where the heat sapped our energy and where our heavy midday meal meant a lazy afternoon. All I knew was the frustration of standing around wasting time when I had bigger ambitions."

"Did you think they were lazy?" Christopher suggests bluntly, provoking me because he knows how I feel about Trinidad. "I sense some *anti-Trini* racism."

I grimace. Trinidad doesn't look or act like Canada, but that has nothing to do with race. It's the crushing climate. Christopher says there are medical schools down in the Caribbean, but I can't fathom how any expatriate could study for their examinations in that heat.

"Did you talk to your father when you went back home?" Christopher asks, using my silence to change the subject.

"He wasn't there! By then, he'd already left for the United States. As soon as I went abroad, he moved away the very next year. I think he stayed in Trinidad just long enough to make my life a living hell. We played chicken until I took the initiative and got out.

"And as soon as he left, the rest of my family emigrated too, one by one. They saw their opportunity. *Get rich in the States*, everyone said. *Good jobs, lots of money*. The point was to leave a Third World country and make your fortune, but Daddy never got one penny richer. He had no ambition, and ended up renting an old, decrepit apartment building in the Bronx for the rest of his miserable life. I used to send money home for my mother, and so did all my sisters and brothers. Everyone did except him."

Christopher nods without fully grasping the tyranny of the frail, benign old man who ended up moaning about his joints and sending strips of limited-edition postage stamps at Christmastime during his last decade.

"Anyway, the stifling predictability of the weather was *boring*. Beautiful and warm today; beautiful and warm tomorrow; beautiful and warm the day after that, right up until the rainy season."

To Canadians shivering in the dark for months, that feeling is incomprehensible. But Canadians underestimate the monotony of wearing the same beach clothes twelve months a year and rarely appreciate their four seasons: the pleasure of leaving the tundra behind for a warm and cozy home, the promise of springtime growth, the anticipation of summer, the recuperation of autumn. Nor are Trinidadians much for gardening: the lots around me were neglected affairs, with parched lawns and withered foliage.

"Back in Port of Spain, they rehired me as a management trainer at the bank. They welcomed me back with open arms. I knew from the start that I wasn't going to stay, figuring I'd be back in Canada within a month. But it took them *nine full months* to approve my landed immigrant visa."

"That visa was a full-term baby," says Christopher. "Were you excited to get it?"

"Yes." No hesitation there. "It meant I could escape from Trinidad again. It was easier this time around. I had some regrets saying goodbye to my mother and sister again – and leaving the bank again – but this time I was on my way to a country I now considered my adopted home, where I would be with my friends again. Remember, I was still dating Leon when I graduated, and I'd left him back in Prince Edward Island. I would have had to wait two more years for him to finish school. And he'd write to me while I was waiting in Trinidad for my visa. He kept asking *where the heck are you*? He couldn't believe I was really gone."

"Did you tell your mom about your white boyfriend?" asks Christopher. "Or did she sniff him out on her own? *Here's another letter from your white devil.*"

I laugh and shrug. "No, Christopher."

"Nobody forced you to come back to Canada," he points out. "You had your degree. You could have climbed higher and higher at that bank in Trinidad. You could have married a nice Black man, and then your kids would have been the same race as you."

"How can you be a different race from me?" I exclaim. "You're my son!"

This time, it's Christopher who shrugs. Since I haven't got the slightest idea what he's on about, I ignore him and continue my story.

## 35. YOUR CALL IS IMPORTANT TO US

My early immigrant experiences lacked high drama, and maybe they won't hold Christopher's attention, but at least he's a captive audience.

"I came back to Toronto in September 1968 and found a job in Accounts Receivable at Proctor & Gamble. The office was all intellectuals, and I exchanged poetry with a coworker whose writing inspired me. But happy as I was, I moved on six months later to Bell Canada – which was even more sprawling a monopoly then than it is now. *Ma Bell*, everybody called it."

"Everyone loves their mother," offers Christopher.

"Bell was listed on Fortune 500 as one of the best companies to work for in Canada, and it was the largest female employer in the country. Unionized, so it paid well. Competitive, because it meant *boundless* opportunities for advancement. I had high expectations when they hired me as an entry-level Service Representative, even if the job itself was nothing special: I arranged phone service for customers moving into or out of the area, discussed their accounts, answered billing questions, and arranged account credits. We communicated with the installation, repair, accounting, and traffic departments, and sent delinquent accounts to collections.

"I was one of four new hires, and after some intensive training, they assigned two of us to the same west end office. Thirty of us, working under this drill sergeant of a woman. Me and Norma, the other new hire, equally traumatized so we became fast friends. We were young and impressionable, but experience gave us the confidence to enjoy our work. We learned tact and diplomacy, because we wanted to give the customer the kind of first experience that made second experiences unnecessary. Our overbearing supervisor always reminded us how critical we were, and how important it was to follow through on promises. She monitored us in-person and remotely, at least until the government banned recording phone conversations without consent."

Christopher fidgets with his watch. I've lost him.

## 36. GREY EYES

"So," says Christopher, changing the subject. "You're in the big city. You must have met plenty of Black men after you graduated. How exciting was that?"

"I never met *any* Black men in Toronto," I retort. "Not in 1967. When I came to Canada, you didn't see Black folks. If you walked by one on the sidewalk, you'd turn and stare."

But Christopher is equally emphatic. "There must have been plenty," he says. "I can look it up if you want. You could have joined *Black* cultural events, or a *Black* community centre, or…some sort of immigrants' association? Wouldn't you have been more comfortable around them? Wouldn't you have shared something with them? What's your problem with *Black men* anyway?"

"I just wasn't interested, Christopher!" I exclaim, interrupting his onslaught before worrying about my composure. Maybe I just admitted I could have found a Black man then, somewhere, if I really wanted to. "Maybe it was the way we all hated our father. I just didn't trust anybody who reminded me of him."

"Didn't stop your sisters. Doesn't stop you insisting I should date Black women."

"No, I keep saying you should date a *mixed* girl," I correct him. Christopher has never brought a white girl home for dinner, despite my insistence that he should date the daughter of his high school mathematics teacher. Statuesque, auburn hair, good and Catholic. But more conspicuously, he's also never brought home a Black girl. Maybe that's my fault.

"That's awfully specific. Really shrivels my dating pool."

"A lot of Black girls are mixed. Black and Indian. Black and Oriental. So many beautiful mixed girls. And then the two of you would have something in common."

"*Asian*, mom. Rugs are Oriental. People are Asian." He pauses, then adds: "I have a virtual date with a Trinidadian girl tonight."

"No, you're making that up. What does she look like?"

"She's pretty. But what do I have in common with a Trinidadian?"

"I'll tell you my real, basic answer," I say carefully. "There's something in the *blood* that attracts *blood*. And even though I dated so many white guys, now I realize I was always missing that Black connection."

"So, if you could go back in time, you'd date Black men?"

"I told you, there were none!"

"*If* you could go back and there *were* Black men, you'd date them?"

"Yah."

"American Black men?" Christopher clarifies.

"Not American Black men," I snap. "But when I was seventeen, there was one guy in Trinidad who liked me. Mulatto with beautiful grey eyes. That was when I was a kid, and it was right before I left to come to Canada. And then, when I came back home to wait for my visa, I met another guy named Allan who was crazy about me. We used to go for walks and that was it, because he was in the middle of a divorce. My Catholic upbringing didn't let me take him seriously, but I could feel a *pull*, and if he'd been single, I would have given him a chance. Like I said, something in the blood, you know?"

"Black men are wilder." Christopher smiles.

"Don't' get me going on the Roberts family," I agree. "They're *all* wild."

## 37. HAZEL EYES

"Anyway, I tore up half of Leon's letters when he got married."

"Why would you do that?"

"I was angry."

"I see."

"Then, after a brief courtship, I married Roger and tore up the other half of Leon's letters. And that was that."

"That's dramatic."

Roger was an immigrant from England. And like me, Canada had lured him with the promise of opportunity back when England was in the throes of post-war recession. He was six-feet tall, one hundred and fifty-five pounds, and white, with hazel eyes and curly-hair. And despite my experiences with Ron and Leon, I had no serious reservations about marrying a white man. I lived and worked entirely among white people, so no surprise I'd marry one.

"What did your father think of that?" asks Christopher, as if it mattered one iota what my father thought.

"He didn't think anything," I reply. "I came to Canada, got my degree, got married, had you, and he was never the wiser. All that time, for ten or fifteen years, we weren't even on speaking terms – at least until he was much older and much sicker."

"Not even for the wedding?" Christopher seems genuinely puzzled, but I'm mostly puzzled by his bewilderment.

"Of course not," I say. "What are you talking about? I told you we weren't even speaking!"

"He must have known about your wedding, if your mother knew."

"Oh, she wouldn't tell him. She knew perfectly well how I felt about him, and nobody would ever take his side. Remember, he had that mistress across town."

## 38. DIVERSITY HIRE

"This isn't about Roger though," I declare. "This is about *Bell Canada*."

"Is it? I'd almost forgotten," says Christopher. He props his face in his hands, restless and resentful of every second he isn't lying on the floor.

"So meanwhile," I continue, "I dove headfirst into all the office socials and got along with *everyone*. They elected me union representative for the Canadian Telephone Employer Association, which gave me a window into personnel problems, management relationships and negotiations, and helped me learn the soft skills of successful meetings. I had to juggle my union responsibilities with my existing duties as a Service Representative.

Over those first three years, the turnover around me was fast and furious. Sometimes, it took under a year of indifferent performance to see a co-worker fast-tracked by management. Often, Norma and I would be baffled by the selection process, especially when their promotion seemed to have little relationship with education or seniority. Everyone was fully aware of each other's job performance and communication skills, so we knew who the real stars were.

The arbitrary promotions caused resentment, hostility, and sometimes, even grievance complaints. The explanations from the top were never good enough – and besides, whoever management had their sights on would be pushed through development programs that made them so qualified for any new opening that they became the logical choice. It was a self-perpetuating cycle and complaining about it through formal channels only aggravated our bitterness and frustration.

"The black box of office politics?" Christopher proposes.

I snort.

"I was patient. My attendance and punctuality were flawless, and my performance reviews were uniformly excellent. I got along with *everybody*, whether they were management or not. When we discussed my future with Bell, I always made my supervisor aware of my ambitions, and that I was interested in a serious career with them. But I had this strange gut feeling that my opportunities were being limited. That I was being held back by invisible strings."

"Although you wouldn't run into that problem nowadays." Christopher rubs his chin and leans forward. "Nowadays, there would be a racial quota for management positions, at least at any corporation with a big enough footprint. Maybe explicit, maybe implicit. Either way, they'd hire the Black candidate over anyone else with the same education. You'd be a shoo-in as the diversity hire."

"Maybe," I say, doubtful this utopia exists. "I'm sure they transcribed *ambitious Black female* in red ink somewhere in my file. I did everything I could. In my second year, I aced a Personnel Administration course at the University of Toronto – Bell Canada always covered educational costs for their employees. I proudly presented them with my certificate, thinking it would finally clear the way for my advancement. I still clung to my innocent belief that hard work and determination would eventually be rewarded with success."

But nothing happened. No one offered me development programs to prepare me for management. The promotions continued around me with monotonous, infuriating regularity. Almost monthly. Apparently, I couldn't recognize what was so obvious to my colleagues. In 1972, after three years and three months of slaving away, Norma and a few other colleagues approached me to ask why I was tolerating this racial discrimination.

"I was *flabbergasted*. I looked around at my office and saw that *not even one* employee was a minority. Maybe I'd been so used to Prince Edward Island, but that's when it finally dawned that there was only one other Negro girl in the entire building, along with one non-white male Service Rep. No Indians, no Asians, no Arabs, no handicapped."

I'd never felt different before, and yet here were my friends insisting I was being penalized based on my skin colour. It took me some time to process this revelation, one that was anchored by the premise that my qualifications and accomplishments all counted for nothing just because I looked different.

"I'd imagine plenty of minorities came to that conclusion back then," says Christopher. "If only there were some sort of…*racism tricorder*…you know, like in *Star Trek*. And you'd wave it around the workplace like a wand. Maybe it would spit out the ambient level of systemic racism like a smoke detector and calculate the precise amount of diversity necessary to correct it."

I ignore him and continue.

"I discussed it with your father. He warned me it would be challenging to prove my co-workers correct. But he assured me of his complete support if I planned to pursue things."

He, too, was a fighter with an interest in Human Rights, and he thought it was at least worth investigating. By now, I had enough experience with Bell to know my union would be useless for this kind of grievance. So, I contacted the provincial Department of Labor instead, and they told me that since Bell Canada operated nationwide, my complaint fell within federal jurisdiction.

That was where my fight began, shadowboxing against a perfectly banal racism that flourishes without anyone bothering to use the word. But even at this point, I didn't need much from Bell Canada. Just a hand up.

## 39. WHEN THE RACISM GETS IN YOUR FACE

"Listen to this one."

Christopher wants a break. He leans fashionably against the kitchen counter, one leg crossed over the other. He's bookmarked a page from *Black Like Me* with his index finger and waits for my full attention.

"Here's a good one," he says. "It's where he shows up in blackface to get a job with *white people*. Imagine, the audacity of showing up to a factory as a minstrel show imitation of a Black person and hoping for the best!"

He reads the passage aloud with mocking high drama, tone swaying high to low like a ship's bow in a tempest:

> "We're gradually getting you people weeded out from the better jobs at this plant. We're taking it slow, but we're doing it. Pretty soon we'll have it so the only jobs you can get here are the ones no white man would have."
> "How can we live?" I asked hopelessly, careful not to give the impression I was arguing.
> "That's the whole point," he said, looking me square in the eyes.

I appease him with a cackle when he gets to the end. He's decided it doesn't sound *authentic*. He doesn't think it's something an actual person would say to another actual person.

"Imagine how much easier life would be if the world

were so transparent," Christopher concludes, closing the book and flinging it onto the counter. "Racism tricorder, I'm telling you."

"I'd have to read it from a different perspective now that I'm mature." I frown. Was I this critical when I read *Black Like Me* in school? Was anyone?

"Because even in your Bell case," Christopher continues, "nobody admitted they were persecuting you because you were Black. Not even Bill Restivo. He didn't lean over the lunch table and whisper, *go back where you came from*. People are cowards like that."

"No, of course not," I say. "Bill wouldn't have dared. And *he was the one* who wouldn't call me back when they were hiring. The whole thing was just too much. Absolute insanity. *Lyris, where are you?* my colleagues would say. *They're hiring people right now! People off the street! People with no experience at all!*"

"Although sometimes," says Christopher, wandering out of the kitchen, "people on the street are the hungriest."

# 40. THE CASE FOR REPARATIONS

Christopher arranges himself on the living room carpet and submits to listening in silence.

"At my last Bell interview," I continue, skipping ahead several years, "the second interviewer was someone who had worked with me for three years on the sales team. By now, he'd been promoted to assistant manager. Just imagine, facing one person I'd worked *with*, and another person I'd worked *for*. And they both acted like they'd never seen me in their life."

"Not even a *welcome back, how's your son?*"

I shake my head, before realizing that's not exactly true.

"They asked me who would look after my son while I worked full-time. It's illegal to ask that now. It was everything, my race, my gender, my marriage. We were juggling so much in that case, and all for nothing. That's what the system is like. By the end, my lawyer was so frustrated she told me my son could grow up, become a lawyer, and take over the case."

"Mom, I'm not doing that."

"Tell me why I shouldn't write Justin Trudeau for an

official apology and reparations. He's giving reparations to *everybody* – the Indigenous for the residential schools, the Muslims, the Inuit, the Italians, *everybody gets an apology*."

"That's just not realistic, mom." Christopher digs his heels in. "You can't demand an official apology from the government for something that's still before the courts. Bell hasn't even acknowledged any wrongdoing."

"They even apologized to the Japanese for the internment camps in the Second World War!" I insist, unsure if I'm being facetious. "Maybe I can get reparations for what they put me through."

Christopher's eyes become wide and bright. Two glistening white balloons ready to burst.

"The other big difference between this and the case for reparations," he says, "is that with reparations, the people who suffered are already good and dead. And the dead are always the most gracious."

## 41. THEY PUT THEIR KNEE ON YOUR NECK

"So why *haven't* you ever written about the Bell case?"

We've migrated back to the den. Christopher is clutching my old journal, a spiral-bound school notebook whose handwritten pages are yellowed, as if kissed by flame. He must have pinched it from the upstairs closet for God knows what purpose, but I don't mind. That journal must be thirty years old, and it ends at the beginning – the beginning of the unpleasantness with Bell and the even greater unpleasantness that followed my departure. Once, I had expected it to be an autobiography, but life rudely interrupted. Besides, who would read such a tome?

"It's so old," I finally say. "It's not fresh in my mind, and I don't know how I would even tackle it. I'm so fed up with it. That journal ends when I left Bell to have a baby and it doesn't even touch on all the trauma to get my job back. That's the end of my story."

"I don't know why that has to be true," says Christopher.

"That's just the way it is," I insist. "Besides, nowadays it's already so *exposed* the way they treat us, what they do to Black people. Everybody already knows they want to keep Black people out of anywhere they can become famous or wealthy. They put their *knee on our neck*."

I'm proud of this. A tribute to the late George Floyd crushed under a white policeman's knee. An homage to the Reverend Jesse Jackson's passionate eulogy. *The reason we could never be who we wanted and dreamed to be is you kept your knee on our neck. It's time for us to stand up in George's name and say get your knee off our necks.* But when he hears my quip, Christopher scrunches his face into a raisin.

"Cringe," he declares. "Mom, can you stop quoting Jesse Jackson long enough to finish the Bell Canada story?"

Predictably, my son never feels the way I do. Maybe he's being contrarian, but I can't understand his reflexive cynicism about the entire Black Lives Matter movement. I've never once heard him say something *positive* about it. It's baffling and disappointing, because with more energy and youth, I'd be on the streets chanting right alongside those crowds of protesters.

Christopher is aware of the Bell ordeal in the form of scattered narrative crumbs I've fed him over the years. But maybe he's never *really* listened, because now he suddenly wants to hear it all again. I appreciate his willingness to hear my experience – but why *now*, I have no idea. Here he is, on the carpet like a child, staring upwards. I brace myself for a tide of scepticism and begin like I always do.

Tangentially.

"Remember me standing at the foot of those skyscrapers in 1967? Taking the staircase up forty-odd stories? Those days, companies registered their vacancies with these employment agencies, who would take care of hiring. One of them gave me a math test – just a simple math test, like I've done a thousand times. I used to get a hundred percent in *every area* of math – calculus, trigonometry, everything. I took their test, and then the woman supervising disappeared into the back room to correct it. She came out later and said *okay, that was fine, we'll let you know.*"

"Uh huh."

"I never questioned her, never said *show me those results*. Just think how innocent I was, that it never crossed my mind."

"What never crossed your mind?"

"That the companies hiring would tell the agencies directly: *don't send us any visible minorities. No Blacks wanted.*

Stuff like that would be *on the file*."

"Are you sure?"

"You think I imagined it? I never went back to put them on the spot. They just never called. And I was too stupid, too innocent to even ask them how long I'd have to wait. Isn't it sad how we never expect other people to be *wicked*?"

"But how can you assume racism," asks Christopher. I tense up even before he finishes the sentence, "when maybe the other students just beat you fair and square on that math test?"

I sniff. Cynicism, right on schedule, like night follows day. Christopher fidgets with his phone, unconvinced. Like I dreamed this up.

"No. And now I know how young and naïve I was. I had no family to say, *don't take this*. Besides, I didn't come to Toronto to make trouble. People just got away with things."

"Even in the end," I continue, "it was my co-workers at Bell who convinced me not to take it. Norma and everyone on the floor who saw what was happening with their *own eyes*. I was in that office three years, watching all those white people sail past me into supervision."

Three years, I whisper to myself, with their *knee on my neck*.

# 42. THE BLACKLIST

That was where I stopped journaling decades ago, instead leaving the convoluted story to professional writers as they saw fit. Somewhere along the way, I became *Anonymous, Toronto* to the pen of a feminist author who reduced my trauma to three short pages among hundreds of other abbreviated biographies. I can't decide whether wedging my entire life into three pages is an accomplishment or an insult.

"All said and done," I continue, "Judith Finlayson interviewed me for a book called *Against the Current*. An anthology of stories about women who had faced gender and racial discrimination. She spent a couple days talking to me, and then asked me to write a few pages summarizing everything in my own words. But when she published her book, she never mentioned Bell by name. That always bothered me. She called them a *large telecommunications company* and left it at that."

"Not surprising," says Christopher. "The case was still before the courts and shaming them might open her up to a libel suit. No starving writer wants any part of that."

"Anyway," I say, "there I was in 1972, a lowly Service Rep, watching all these people push past me one by one into management. It was too much to take. Norma and *ten* of my colleagues instigated a racial discrimination complaint with the Human Rights Commission and testified on my behalf. The Commission marched into the Bell Office to investigate. And *poof*, three months later, I'm miraculously in management. They assigned me my own team of eight reps to supervise. And the Commission followed up with a letter congratulating me on settling my complaint."

"Where's the letter now?" asks Christopher.

"No idea." I rack my brain: had I kept it? It never seemed important at the time. "Maybe I threw it away."

"Thought you'd frame it. That's like throwing away your diploma."

"Right, but I don't think I knew Bell was the problem then." I thought this was a one-off, just a bump in the road. But the discrimination didn't end there – it just mutated. Even though they grudgingly put me in management, I felt like an outsider, and the other supervisors never accepted me."

"They were probably pissed," Christopher says. "If they wanted to promote you on purpose, they would have done it themselves, without the Human Rights Commission elbowing in."

"Of course, they were pissed. They'd have a secret staff meeting every week, and they'd never tell me when they were holding it or what changes they were rolling out. So, I had nothing to tell my reps. They cut me out of the loop completely, and it wasn't fair to the staff under me."

"Weren't you copied on the email chain though?"

"What's email?" I exclaim. "It was word of mouth! They'd whisper to each other: *We're having a meeting at four-thirty*. And after a few months, I couldn't take it anymore. They ostracized me. They'd blacklisted me, and that's when I walked out. You can only take so much, and I didn't want to give myself a stress ulcer."

"That's no way to treat the diversity hire," Christopher agrees. "Sounds like the other supervisors resented the complaint. Maybe they thought you didn't deserve to be where you were. You were that complainer who didn't know her place."

"You mean, I was a *Black* woman who didn't know her place," I correct him. "They didn't give me the information I needed to do my job, Christopher. I was learning. They taught me there was no place in management for someone with my skin colour. Eventually, I gave up, and decided there was no use fighting. I left and returned to my old position as a Service Rep. And then, shortly afterwards, I went back to the Bell employment office to look for other opportunities. And the woman there told me, *you'll do well in sales.*"

I was reluctant at first because selling was man's work. But before I knew it, I found myself in a sales office filled with men.

## 43. ON HAGIOGRAPHY

*'A dart and a laurel for Bell Canada'* is nowhere to be found on the Google even when Christopher adds the publication date: January 1988. He's searched six ways from Sunday, and I can't understand where it's hiding. I thought every word ever printed was filed in perpetuity, and my human rights case was big news, front-page in the Toronto Star's *Life* section. The Star is our newspaper of record, and their archived coverage of the moon landing isn't nearly so hard to find.

"Always that same woman on the byline, this Doris

Anderson character," says Christopher, abandoning his phone to inspect my tattered newspaper clipping. "Why was she so obsessed with the case?"

"She was my writer," I answer. "She has her own chapter in *Against The Current* too. And my lawyer Mary Eberts has another chapter."

"Hagiography," Christopher blurts out. Word of the day. He folds the newspaper clipping and slides it back into the portfolio I loan to anyone curious about my Bell battle. Then he looks up and waits.

"What?"

"It's a word I just learned. It means the biography of a saint, but it more often describes an adulatory or idealized form of writing, when one's primary purpose is to flatter and avoid any hard questions."

"I see. Hagiography?"

"Hagiography. I'm always suspicious when I hear one side of a story. It's always missing a critical piece. I never believe anything until I get to cross-examine."

"So, you think Judith Finlayson's book is a hagiography?"

"She's a feminist, writing about feminists. The book serves her own purposes. First, the premise that women are being held back. Probably true, but never mind. She's already decided her truth, and now she just needs enough examples to fill an anthology. Nuance would be counterproductive. Otherwise, she'd have to call it *Against the Current (and One Woman Who Got What She Deserved)*."

"You can be very cynical."

"I prefer realistic."

# 44. IN WHICH KEN NEEDS THE MONEY

"Let's hear your side of it, then."

"Fine," I say. "What I learned from that first experience was that apparently, there was no place for a Black woman in management."

Many of my colleagues had been approached about moving into sales, but I'd never been asked. I pushed for two more years, and finally, that sympathetic woman in personnel helped me make the move. That's where I spent the next three years. For two of them, I was my division's top performer, one of the top four in our area and a member of the Director's Club.

"My performance appraisal called me *the model other sales reps should follow.*" I pause for dramatic effect. Sales isn't easy, but success is a numerical business, no room for nuance. Even Christopher nods approvingly. He seems impressed.

"Didn't you tell me one client said that if you made it to his door, you must be head and shoulders above any white salesperson?"

"I still remember his name," I say. "Craig Hind. I went to his Dodge dealership in 1979 to make recommendations for his business. When I arrived, he said to me: *You're a Black woman, so for them to send you to my company I know you must be twice as good as the next guy*. He said that right to my face. And I thanked him for the kind words and then got to work evaluating his telephone system. But even though my sales performance was superior, I always felt like my supervisor resented me."

"Bill Restivo," Christopher clarifies. "Your nemesis."

"Yes, Bill Restivo. He'd make snide remarks about me driving to work in a Mercedes. Then, when I had the top sales in my group, he gave the performance bonus to a man. It didn't matter that I was carrying *fifty percent* of the sales load out of *seven* reps. I was pulling half the work, and Bill still gave that $2500 award to Ken Gingrich, even though Ken had twenty five percent less sales than me. That's another name I can't forget. And so, I confronted Bill Restivo in his office."

"Mmmhmm."

"He said it was because Ken had maxed out his Mastercard, and because *you're* driving a Mercedes. He said I didn't need the money. How do I argue with that?"

"In 1979? You tell him *that's communism*, I guess."

"Especially when it was true," I say, ignoring his quip. "Maybe I didn't need the money – your father had a successful business, and we were doing well – but that had nothing to do with my performance. I concluded that the combination of my success and the success of my prosperous, white husband must have bothered him. I think he decided I was a Black woman who didn't know her place."

"Maybe," says Christopher. "But how does somebody even begin to prove that? How can racism be something you just feel in your heart?"

"Come on, Christopher." I'm irritated. "What else

could it be?"

He considers this.

"I mean, when you're convinced that you're dealing with a racist, it shows up in your behaviour, your body language, your tone, your *insinuations*. The other person feels the tension, like pheromones, but they can't explain it. All they can do is react. I barely understand why any two people get along *at the best of times*. And if someone doesn't connect with me, I blame my personality and social skills before my skin colour.

"And whether you're right or wrong," he continues, "it's a self-fulfilling prophecy. How does somebody warm up to someone who resents them? Maybe I'm wondering if you and Bill Restivo were just *common enemies* locked in a cycle of mutual animosity?"

I hate when he does this.

"Sometimes I don't know where I went wrong with you. You aren't an empathetic, supportive ear. You don't *commiserate*."

# 45. IF NOBODY ELSE HAS MY NUMBER

*Word of the day* has mushroomed to unpleasant proportions.

"I think what you're talking about, mom, is what the kids call *intersectionality*."

"What?" I say blankly. "I don't know where you come up with these words."

"The first thing to know about intersectionality," continues Christopher, "is the number of syllables. Seven! But second, I want to know how you ended up leaving sales in the first place. Because if you were a man, I bet you never would have left at all."

"Yah," I begin. "In 1980, I got pregnant with you. Bell allowed new mothers a year of maternity leave, and I took full advantage. But while I was at home with you, I became so attached that I didn't want to go back to work immediately. So, I wrote to my boss and asked for permission to extend my leave for an extra year."

That wasn't unheard of – a male employee took a leave of absence around the same time to run for political office.

Bell gave him indefinite leave for years and then he eventually returned to his original job.

"But when I asked for that extra year, they must have thought *now we have the perfect excuse to get rid of her*. At the end of the second year, I told them I was ready to come back. But rather than offering me my old job, Bill Restivo told me to apply again at the employment office. And that's what I did. I went right down to Bell and filled out an application, and of course, nothing happened."

"Right," offers Christopher. "You'd given yourself away as a Black female who wasn't afraid to use her uterus. You'd already used it once, and you were liable to use it again. A uterus is the most dangerous *intersection* of all."

"All I know is I waited and waited," I continue, ignoring this jargon. "My colleagues in sales all knew how badly I wanted to come back, and they were surprised I hadn't been contacted because they knew Bell was actively hiring. It took ages, but after some persistence, they finally called me for an interview. Turns out the reason for the long delay was that they hadn't been able to find my number. Imagine, the telephone company *couldn't find my phone number*! Christopher, I don't know why they weren't laughed out of court. If nobody else has my number in this entire world, Bell Canada has it."

## 46. THE INTERVIEW

Here's the next part:

"I already told you this part."

"The interview?"

"That strange interview the following week. The interviewing team was Bill Restivo and that newly promoted manager who had worked with me as a sales rep. Both men acted like they'd never laid eyes on me before. Bill Restivo claimed Bell didn't keep old performance reviews, and maybe he hadn't kept his memory either."

"Eyesight fades with age, you know."

"I arrived expecting the interview to take fifteen minutes – after all, I'd worked there for eleven years, and they knew me. Instead, they dragged it out over two hours. *How do you feel about being sent out of town three or four days a week?* they asked me. That never happens, at least not in all the time I'd worked for them, and you ask this of a woman you're perfectly aware just came back from maternity leave? *What do you remember as the worst part of the job?* What kind of bizarre question is that?"

"Intersections," Christopher responds. "They were worried you'd disappear into the intersection again to make more babies."

"Uh huh," I say. "I think that's exactly what they thought. They badgered me with the kinds of questions that left me feeling like I was a stranger, and when the interview was over, my whole body felt cold. Everything about it felt ominous. And of course, no sooner had I arrived home than the employment office called to tell me I didn't get the job. Thanks for coming out, but I wasn't a *perfect match* for my old position. Why wouldn't they rehire me? In those eleven years, not only did I have stellar performance reviews, but also perfect attendance and punctuality. They'd given me a plaque and a silver tray. Ten absence-free years!"

"Maybe they thought you'd outgrown the job. Or the opposite, that you were rusty."

"Right," I say. "I was the kind of employee any company would be eager to have back. But instead, they rejected me. I couldn't see any explanation other than racial discrimination.

I decided I wouldn't let them deprive me of my job, so I called the Human Rights Commission again. And after reviewing the evidence, they agreed to hear my case."

Christopher frowns.

"Racism by process of elimination?"

"You tell me, what else could it be?" I snap. "I was their top performer. Instead of saying *No blacks wanted*, this time all they had to say was, *there isn't a perfect match between you and the job*."

"I guess," shrugs Christopher. "What else could it be? Well, sexism for one."

"Uh huh." I'm satisfied hearing his resistance crumble, saving face by replacing one *ism* for another. "My lawyer prepared an argument accusing Bell of discrimination based on gender as well as race. If I'd been a man, I wouldn't have taken maternity leave in the first place, and my leave of absence gave them the perfect chance to weed me out. My lawyer thought ageism might have been a factor too – since they didn't hire any new sales reps in my age bracket. Don't take my word for it: their interview questions were all *right there* too, plain as you could see, and so were my answers."

# 47. MA BELL CALLING

"So maybe, all Bell really wanted was an unbroken line-up of white male sales reps," says Christopher. "Although if they stuck you right in the *middle* of the holiday photo, it wouldn't even mess up the symmetry."

I laugh picturing this, all while racking my brain to recall even one other woman or person of colour on that sales team.

"Almost immediately," I continue, "I knew Bell planned to stonewall. They had vaults of money to keep the legal appeals going until the end of time, figuring I'd get tired and drop it. That was their strategy, and it was a good one. The Human Rights case went on so long I lost track of what was being appealed and why."

"Solid plan," says Christopher. "Did you keep souvenirs of all the case files?"

"Are you kidding? Come on."

I beckon, and Christopher follows me downstairs into the basement, slinging his canvas backpack over his shoulder. We enter a white room bleached by harsh fluorescent lights that flicker and hum like a wasp's nest. It was an office once upon a time when I was married, but now the walls are new-home bare save for the stacks of folders strewn across the far corner.

Beside those folders lays a coffee-coloured suitcase, and I bend to unlock the brass buckles. Inside, collated bundles of miscellaneous documents beckon – everything from those front-page articles in the *Life* section of the Star, to completed and abandoned Sudoku puzzles from interminable court sessions, to an old Bell performance review dating from 1978, to a loose-leaf photocopy of a meme entitled *All I ever needed to know, I learned in kindergarten*.

"This is what I carried with me when I sat in on the court cases. I'd take my little briefcase with me."

"It's a *go-bag*." Christopher chews his lower lip and sifts through the pages. "They thought your language skills were *excellent*," he says, reading from one performance review. "That's a microaggression. You can't tell people of colour that they're articulate anymore."

I frown.

"If you express surprise at a Black person's language skills," he says, "it sends the message that you expected them to be *in*articulate. But overall, Bell gave you top marks. They say you *handled more complex accounts* in 1980."

When he reaches my legal transcripts, he scans the title pages and deftly slides the files into the back pocket of his backpack. Maybe he expected I wouldn't notice.

"How come you want to take so much stuff off of me?" I demand to know, squinting. Christopher shrugs and continues leafing through the tome.

"Piles here, piles there, more piles in cold storage. Piles this high." I separate my hands a vertical foot.

"Fat lot of good it did you," says Christopher, coming across a piece of correspondence bearing Bell Canada letterhead, addressed to a niche magazine called *Human Rights Advocate*. "Look, here's a good one."

Your July edition of the Human Rights Advocate carries an article on Lyris Dainton, a former employee of Bell Canada who charges the company with discrimination, claiming she has been refused her previous sales position based on sex and race.

Because the case is still before the Canadian Human Rights Commission, we do not feel at liberty to discuss the case in your publication. We would point out, however, that if we were being discriminatory based on sex and race, how did Lyris Dainton get hired in the first place and have a series of promotions leading to the sales department position?

In short, what bothers us about your story is its tone of guilt on the part of the company even though the facts are still to be determined in an investigation. Surely there are enough cases that have been fully investigated and the verdict in for you to write about, rather than writing one-sided pieces where only one party provides information, and the other is automatically condemned.

Yours truly,

MV James
Information Director for Public Affairs

"Savage," says Christopher, handing me the letter. "They're treating you like a lunatic. But at least you got their attention."

"Mmmhmm. And then they referred the journalist at the *Advocate* to a 122-page transcript of the court hearing from the previous June. And after that, it was another full year of delay, where nothing moved an inch in court."

"Wasn't Bell a monopoly back then?" Christopher frowns. "What do they care about bad press?"

"I can't remember if that was before or after they had competition," I say. "All I know is Bell never offered me *one iota* more than they were forced to. I had top-notch performance. I busted my butt for them. But I had to beg or make waves to get anything. In those days, nobody was talking about systemic racism the way they do now."

"So, you admit they couldn't get away with it now," says Christopher, with the hint of a smile. "They'd bend over backwards to hire you now."

"Of course, they wouldn't get away with it now. But back then, I had about six different human rights officers investigating my complaint over one period of eighteen months. The file got passed from one to the next. When they transferred one officer away from Toronto, he asked me if I would drop my complaint so he could clear up his desk. And in the end, the Commission wasn't as thorough as it should have been when they compiled the evidence. Nothing in the file about my first discrimination complaint with Bell, which you'd think might have helped establish a pattern of behaviour."

"And through the whole thing, I kept job hunting. It took *four more years* to find another job. It was demoralizing, and I wondered if I'd been blacklisted. Then, after seven years of bickering in the courts, I couldn't continue: mom died back in Trinidad, and I was getting divorced from your father. I had too much on my plate to deal with Bell anymore."

"It couldn't have helped with the letter of reference from your last employer," admits Christopher. "They might have mentioned offhand that you'd sued them twice. That wouldn't be too helpful. *Lyris is a hard worker, enthusiastically pursuing her ongoing litigation with the same tenaciousness as she approached her role in sales.*"

"Yah, exactly," I say. "So, that's what happened – my side of it anyway. In the end, I still think women who are victims of discrimination should fight, but my experience made me lose all faith in the justice system. I remember we had a junior lawyer working as an assistant on my case – the top graduate in her class – and after four years watching the Bell case play out, she left the profession completely. She was disillusioned. She said if law was the art of obstructing justice, then she wanted no part of it. She knew I had an excellent case, an outstanding lawyer, and the support of the Human Rights Commission – and yet, I couldn't win. If this was our legal system, then how does anyone get justice?"

"The truth is when David fights Goliath," says Christopher. "Goliath always wins, except that one time in the Bible."

"I still feel guilty. I wanted to apologize to that woman who sacrificed her whole career on my account. I wish she knew what she was getting herself into before they called her to the bar. Imagine how much time and money she would have saved herself."

# 48. ANATOMY OF A CASE STUDY

One more thing.

"And then," I say, securing the brass buckles of the briefcase, "the Law Society of Canada had the *nerve* to write me a letter asking if they could use my lawsuit as a case study for students. I asked them *why*. To prove what? To show them how one day they too can lose excellent cases? To turn them off from becoming lawyers? I said *no*, nobody's getting their hands on this until the case is finished."

We retreat up the staircase in silence. That's all I have to say about Bell. Reopening the briefcase is like lifting away a still life painting of a fruit bowl to expose the rot and cracked drywall beneath. Somewhere in that backpack, Christopher has taken possession of those court transcripts, the record of how Bell Canada unchained its attack dog, who lunged at me with jaws dripping with contempt. To think I listened to that man deliver Pierre Trudeau's eulogy, feigning the polished sophistication of the white progressive.

"Maybe the law students could have acted out the court transcript in small breakout groups," Christopher says at the landing. "One of them could play Roy Heenan, and another one could play Mary Eberts."

But he looks reflective, like all this has made him consider something else. He waits until we're back in the den before putting his thoughts into words:

"I wonder what Abagbe Adebayo would say about this. Maybe this is that *systemic racism* everybody is talking about."

# PART THREE

# 49. REASONABLE DOUBT

Maybe it all happened just like she says.

I'm cross-legged on the floor of the den. In the kitchen, my mother is on the phone with her sister, chattering in a Broadway stage whisper. Trying to be discreet, but I can distinguish every laboured syllable.

"I think he's writing a book about me," I hear her say. "Or about Black history, or Trinidad, or the Bell case, or something. He's been asking so many questions. And if he is writing a book, he would never tell me until it's finished. But it's all just a little too suspicious."

She says this, and I'm holding two court transcripts. The first one alone is 122-pages long. Attached to each tome, chronologies of events, meticulous legal minutiae, and executive summaries of investigative reports. It's overwhelming. She's right that I'm writing a book, and she needs to overcome her struggle by the time sixty-thousand words roll around. It's my job to make that happen. So, I randomly open the obnoxious mass of stapled pages and find a report apparently filed on May 26, 1986. I scan through the copious ink.

The investigator's report substantiates the position that Bell Canada has maintained, i.e., The complaints are totally unsubstantiated and should have been dismissed without the lengthy proceedings.

I feel a lump in my throat. Two cruel words swim into and out of focus. *Totally unsubstantiated*.

Reasonable doubt.

It doesn't take much to sow it. Doubt, a dandelion seed puff drifting into a pristine bed of roses. Doubt, the freshly waxed floor where they found the body. Did he slip? Hard to say. Doubt, the security camera footage where the rape victim hugs and laughs with the accused. Was she asking for it? Of course not. Doubt, the supposed nano-thermites under the ruined Twin Towers.

Maybe this Bell business was all just a mistake.

Maybe it was arrogant to convince myself that my cursory inspection was more diligent than the work of Bell Canada and its crack legal team. That my silly three paragraph letter could weigh against this immense file and now, this investigator's report dismissing my mother's allegations as not just unsubstantiated but *totally unsubstantiated*? That the rotting plank I threw across two rocks could be called a suspension bridge.

I'm deflated.

I don't know how to arrest my doubts, stop them from spreading like that dandelion puff in a cynical world of uncharitable people, toxic chat rooms, and hostile comment sections. I'm not naïve: I'm convinced that a third of the rabble will parrot any slogan, intoxicated by tribal consensus, while another third – the contrarians – will believe nothing, even defy overwhelming evidence. They're equally drunk on being the smartest ones in the room. On a good day, that leaves one final third who might be sympathetic to an ironclad case that doesn't buckle under *reasonable doubt*.

In other words, what good is any of this if I can't simultaneously be fair to a nebulous entity called Bell Canada, to a flawed human called Bill Restivo, and to my own beloved mother? She deserves better than thinly veiled condescension and false validation. Maybe that's the best I can do.

## 50. THE DEVIL'S AVOCAT

Everyone knows the *straw man*, but maybe not the *steel man*.

In Philosophy 101, we learned the straw man is the flimsiest, most impotent construction of your adversary's position. He's the piñata of disingenuousness you slap together just to beat the stuffing out of it. He's a crude caricature of Bill Restivo, dressed in freshly laundered white robes, tiki torch in hand as he sets fire to the enormous burning cross staked to my mother's lawn. Cell phone in one hand, noose in the other, our straw villain calls the Bell Canada head office as flames dance and flicker in the moonlight, casting lopsided shadows over his coal-black eyes.

*It's done*, he announces.

*That man*, my mother declares with confidence, *is a racist*.

With clean lines, simple motives, and a crow's-path between cause and effect, the straw man is plot perfect. It's the version I like best because I'm on my mother's side. For her sake, I'd rather Bell Canada represent an Orwellian boot stomping on a Black face – forever.

But life is never so simple, and that's when the *steel man* knocks. Good people do bad things, and so do upstanding corporate entities. Doing bad things was easier when bad things were acceptable, and it's not fair to judge a 1980s workplace by today's exacting standards. But even contemplating this leaves a bitter taste. Nobody likes balance. Nobody likes the steel man.

The steel man is your adversary in his finest form, his rebuttal delivered without even a hint of mocking lilt. The steel man is the counterargument your adversary would articulate himself, presented as living proof that you perfectly empathize with his perspective. After presenting an adequate steel man, your words would be met with satisfied silence. Your adversary would open and close his mouth, fish-like, then uncross his arms:

*I couldn't have said it better myself. Finally, you get it.*

For Bell Canada's steel man, meet Roy Heenan, whose obituary I find in the 2017 Montreal Gazette. *Roy Heenan, legal giant and founding partner of Heenan Blaikie, dead in his eighty-second year, husband of fifty-one years, beloved father and grandfather, expert on employment law, founding chairman of the Pierre Elliott Trudeau Foundation, and Officer of the Order of Canada.* Known for his enthusiasm, humour and generosity, Roy Heenan was beloved by all but my mother.

Roy Heenan, the celebrity attorney assigned the singular and unenviable task of undermining her credibility. The rooster whose legs Bell fitted with razorblades, then released into the courts in a flurry of feathers and squawks. Who can blame him? Everybody deserves a vigorous defence, and sometimes the vigour is the point. Sometimes, the spectacle of obstruction and opposition are all that matter. The real person behind the case and her personal experience are lost, nothing more than collateral damage.

No. That's unfair. Sneaky sarcasm, sinister disguise for just another straw man.

## 51. THE DARK REIGN OF DACE

Before Roy Heenan, however, was Dace Philips. I find her obituary in a 2014 page from the *Toronto Star*, her death following a short battle with cancer.

She's white, with a bowl of short, silver hair encircling a roundish, everywoman face. Her crinkled laugh lines and bright, kind eyes shine through frameless glasses.

> ...determined, intelligent, and passionate...a force of nature and an inspiration. She radiated kindness and compassion. A lifelong learner, she excelled at everything...

I need a ruthless villain, and maybe the obituaries were a poor place to start.

> Dace trail-blazed an impressive career at Bell Canada, demonstrating business acumen and versatility. She was multilingual speaking five languages...

I stop reading once her obituary has confirmed that Dace makes a better candidate for knighthood than fairy-tale scoundrel. However, a chunk of that sparkling career at Bell involved aggressively investigating my mother's discrimination complaint in her role as Regional Director of Labour Relations. It takes me the better part of a day to dig through the hundreds of piecemeal legal documents, chronologies, and other correspondence I've borrowed – but in the end, I manage to construct an elaborate mental image of the late Dace Philips, labouring passionately inside a beige cubicle buried somewhere deep within that grey fortress.

In the summer of 1980, the telephone industry was in turmoil, having been recently upended by the Canadian Radio-television Commission to allow for competition. Now without its monopoly, Bell decided it wanted sales specialists with *proven skills, high motivation, and a track record of success in an extremely competitive environment.*

Bell felt employees who had worked for them in the past hadn't been adequately exposed to this new, cutthroat environment, so they began looking at high-performing people with somewhat different experience. Dace acknowledged that the strength of my mother's past performance was self-evident. But that was then. The new Bell already had a fresh list of eligible sales candidates, and a surplus of hungry, ambitious employees in 1982 and the first quarter of 1983. No room at the inn.

"When L. Dainton insisted we interview her, we did so in August 1983," wrote Dace, pointing out that resumé screening wasn't even done by the same managers who interviewed her. "Her insistence first led us to believe we had in her a candidate who would show high levels of interest and motivation for a sales career in a highly competitive environment."

But they were wrong.

Dace connected with my mother's two interviewers, followed by an employment representative, a manager, multiple sales representatives, and a clerk. Her summary report in February 1986 concluded, based on the interview notes, that L. Dainton was less interested in sales, and more interested in insinuating her way into a career in the personnel department. And although their assessment contradicted all her previous performance appraisals, her Bell interviewers had been unimpressed by the latest two hours they had spent in her company. They had written that my mother preferred *orderliness and neatness to change* and that, unfortunately for her, the current industry was *in a state of flux*.

In the end, the sales team hired ten men and two women that year. Those included seven hires in their twenties, five in their thirties, and none in their forties. Bell also rehired one woman who, like my mother, had a young child at home. Nothing to see here, move along.

Dace also wanted to set the record straight on the disputed Performance Award. My mother hadn't been the only one labouring under the mistaken impression that anyone who inhaled the rarefied air of Director's Club status automatically received the sales performance award – only one employee correctly identified that the award was sometimes given to junior employees as *positive reinforcement*. Dace clarified that in 1979, forty-four of the winners hadn't made the Director's Club at all. And besides, it was a *group* of sales managers, not a lone moustache-twirling renegade, who came to a consensus on who would receive the award.

The Human Rights Commission followed up by appointing its own investigator and conciliator to help negotiate a settlement. Their emissary, Bart Sackrule, burst onto the scene aiming to restore my mother's sales position, recover her lost wages and benefits, and secure compensation for any injury to her self-respect. But in his report, he instead recommended *that the complaints be dismissed because, on the evidence, the allegation of discrimination is unfounded.* Not surprisingly, Bell took this victory and ran with it, flatly rejecting all the proposed terms of settlement.

Pleased with her unexpected win, Dace wrote one final

letter to the Commission.

"We agree with the recommendation to dismiss the complaints after a very lengthy and time-consuming investigation," she responded, adjusting her spectacles upward with an index finger. "We also want to identify that during the investigation it became quite apparent that the complainant was abusing the rights provided to all individuals under the Canadian Human Rights Act, by raising multiple grounds for investigation without reasonable grounds for such allegations so easily made. This is obvious from the admissions implicit in her position that she *was not sure as to the exact reason* and that *I seem to have exhausted all the possibilities but racial discrimination.*"

Having expelled this devastating sentence from her typewriter, but without harbouring any personal malice towards my mother, our villain Dace Philips stood inside her cubicle, stretched her arms in satisfaction, pushed in her office chair, and returned home to her loving family.

## 52. UNCLE TOM'S CUBICLE

"What about this guy from the Commission who threw you under the bus?" I ask my mother delicately as she walks me towards the train station. "The investigator, Bart Sackrule. The double agent. Him and Dace Philips both seemed to think you were abusing the Human Rights process. And then Bell took their report and used it against you."

"Oh, I remember him. He was a Black man. And I think he was a traitor."

"He was Black?"

That surprises me, because unlike Roy Heenan and Dace Philips, Bart Sackrule is a phantom as far as the internet is concerned. Aside from a neglected Facebook page bearing the blurry image of a man standing in a wheatfield, I can't find any trace of him.

"Well, kind of a mix," she clarifies. "You could tell he had some Negro in him. But not enough, because nobody else on my case could figure out how that investigation fell through."

I see where she's going with this. Bart Sackrule was

someone like me. Kind of a mix. Congenitally sceptical and searching for the impossible: that unassailable smoking gun, the overt evidence of covert discrimination. But maybe he was a race traitor – that, too, is impossible to know.

"And all the time, he was talking to me *nice-nice*, and we all thought there was something fishy about him. As though he couldn't tell my complaint was justified. It was *open and shut*, Christopher. They strung the case out until I had no more energy left to fight them."

"Right. But I guess he concluded you were bothering the Human Rights Commission with complaint after baseless complaint. Wasting everybody's time."

"There's a word for that," says my mother, "for that kind of busybody who bothers the courts again and again with frivolous lawsuits."

"*Vexatious complainant*, I think."

"As if I'd do this for fun. There's a word for that, too. For Bart Sackrule, for Black faces who aren't Black voices, Christopher."

I laugh, because for once the aspersion isn't being cast back at me. "You mean, an Uncle Tom?"

# 53. THE JUMPING OFF POINT

Shortly after, my mother wrote an eloquent six-page letter to the Human Rights Commission in response to Bart Sackrule's recommendation. She pointed out several inaccuracies and inconsistencies and posed several rhetorical follow up questions.

"What was the chain of events when ex-employees Kirsten Shunk and Mary Saunders were rehired?" she prodded. "Their performance, tenure and dedication when they worked with me were demonstrably inferior."

Under the bus you go. It's harsh but fair.

She also claimed some of her interview questions had bordered on entrapment, not to mention their responses had been wilfully misinterpreted.

"During the interview, Bill Restivo mentioned that his sister had a baby and returned to work with a couple days off a week," she said, "and I reacted by saying she had arranged a nice compromise." Not that it would be any of Bell's business either way, she might have added.

She went on to point out that Bart Sackrule's challenge had been in finding something called a *jumping off point*. In her conversations with an aide, as late as April 1983, he had informed her that he would be personally recommending the case be sent to a Human Rights Tribunal. My mother demanded to know what had happened between then and the following month, when Bart Sackrule submitted a final report suggesting exactly the opposite.

She concluded by baiting the Commission, rejecting the recommendation, complaining that it *encourages any employer who wants to practice covert discrimination and escape with impunity, so long as they haven't left direct written or verbal evidence.* This report didn't ask the right questions of Bell, nor challenge their contradictory responses.

Circular reasoning, maybe. The essential property of covert discrimination is its invisibility. Knives are sharp, soup is wet. As the internet trolls say: *hmmm, yes, the floor here is made of floor*. Either way, in February 1987, the Commission formally ignored Bart Sackrule and called for a Tribunal anyway. In her blunt rejection, Hanne Jensen, the director of complaint and compliance, wrote back to Bell, explaining that my mother's demonstrated superior performance in

1979 (and commitment to the sales job) established a *prima facie* case. Whether Bell's explanations were defence enough would best be determined by a Tribunal.

*Prima facie* is Latin for *on first sight*. It means that at face value, my mother's grievance had enough merit to justify having a judge haggle over the particulars. With this stinging defeat, Dace Philips might have hurled a lamp at her cubicle wall in a fulsome fit of fury and frustration. No way to know. Bare minimum, she must have frowned deeply.

"We were surprised that the recommendation to dismiss the complaints as unfounded was not accepted by the Canadian Human Rights Commission," wrote Dace upon returning from the water cooler. "The recommendation to settle the matter to the mutual advantage of all parties is unacceptable. The Company did not discriminate against L. Dainton in the decision not to re-hire and consequently sees no reason to settle the complaints."

Having written this, and harbouring no specific malice towards my mother, our villain Dace Philips once more returned home to her loving family.

## 54. EBERTS V. HEENAN, LIVE AT THE RENAISSANCE

Drown long enough in court transcripts and maybe you splash to the surface in that very courtroom. Whether daydream, nightmare, or literary device, I can *see* it clearly as the glass towers outside my window. Whatever the outcome, my mother had awakened a slumbering giant and goaded it into hiring one of Canada's most legendary legal teams to fight back. Billable hours. Paralegals. Correspondence launched by bicycle courier and flung back by the same means.

I assume, anyway. Foolish to expect to understand the complexities of the law without a lawyer. A doctor fumbling through legal records is like a lawyer extracting an appendix with pliers.

"Avani, help, this is consuming me," I type, before resting my phone beside me. *Do not disturb*. Back to work. Back to the original complaint, filed December 12, 1983:

> The Complainant alleges she was not rehired in September 1983 by the Respondent as a sales representative because of her race, colour, national or ethnic origin, age, sex, and family status.

I turn the page and my fantasia begins, the rows of black ink blurring into a chain link fence of unbroken text, then one continuous grey wall, legalese, rebuttals, each speaker's identity betrayed by a terse page header. My eyelids were already heavy, but now I've reread the same line without comprehension. I can't tell how long I've been reading it, nor how many times I've reread it before I surface in a courtroom inside the Scarborough Renaissance Hotel, its colours muted and sharp edges now soft. Dreamlike.

It's early morning on June 26, 1987, and my mother enters the salon to meet her counsel, Mary Eberts and Audrey Macklin. She smiles briefly, welcoming hands connect, and then she takes her place beside them at the counsel table.

In parallel, Roy Heenan and Dace Phillips trade notes. What remains of Heenan's receding hairline is chaotic, a crown of stray salt and pepper hairs misdirected here and there like wheat strands on a windswept plain. Above them on the high ground of the bench waits the Tribunal Chairman, oblivious to the last-minute frenzy of the peasants in the village.

Mary Eberts' impeccable demeanour is crowned by a short bob. She rests two fingers on her chin, staring straight ahead with expectant eyebrows, as if posing for the cover of the law school admissions brochure. She nods as Audrey whispers in her ear.

Just after nine-thirty, Roy Heenan jumps to his feet, a voluminous and rumpled grey jacket set against an uninspired white button-up shirt. His crimson necktie is crooked as a motel picture frame.

He says he should clarify some housekeeping matters before his friend delivers her opening statement, and the Chairman allows it.

"There are two separate objections," begins Heenan, deliberate in his articulation. Mischievous eyes give him the wily look of an oversized squirrel, and his lips curl into what could be mistaken for a vague smile. "But I will start with the first. The first is *confusion*, because depending on whether we're basing ourselves on the question of race or colour or sex, the defences will be quite different. We suffer from a multiplicity of causes. A little of this, a little of that and if something here doesn't stick, well, maybe something over here will, and I don't think that's how we should proceed."

Full stop. Heenan turns on his heels and returns to his seat, flattening his wrinkled jacket against his sides.

"Ms. Eberts, your opening statement?" says the Chairman, nodding to my mother's counsel table.

Two fingers descend from Mary Eberts' chin, and she stands to groom her own jacket against her waist.

"The three grounds of race, colour, and ethnic origin are all of a piece," she begins, leaving a strategic pause before diving in: "Her sex and family status are as bound up with one another as are race, colour, and ethnic origin. These descriptive words are *completely coextensive* within Mrs. Dainton."

Another pause, letting her words settle like dust.

"Of the twelve employees hired in 1983," she continues, "five applied after Mrs. Dainton and had no record of competitive sales. Furthermore, in her interview, Mrs. Dainton gave answers which demonstrated her readiness to get back into competitive sales. The impact of those answers was either ignored or minimized."

"Here was a person of superior achievement and a long

track record with Bell who indicated a willingness to get back into this position and she was turned down. One then asks, what is the reason? Well, first, consider the context: the evidence of an earlier successful complaint against Bell for race discrimination that was resolved in 1972."

"Bell couldn't have fired her and possibly couldn't have forever passed her over for promotion because she had an outstanding record. It would have taken extraordinary, probably improper efforts to remove her. But once she was out of that niche for family reasons and had to reapply, the stage was set for some quite discretionary and discriminatory attitudes. The question is: should a Black woman from Trinidad enjoy this level of success or should she settle for more modest aspirations?"

"It will be our thesis that the absence of any rational explanation for Bell's conduct towards Mrs. Dainton, coupled with her supervisor's attitude towards her, point to discrimination being a factor in Mrs. Dainton's denial of re-hire."

# 55. MA BELL STRIKES BACK

She sits, and the Chairman nods to Heenan.

"I'm glad my friend called it a thesis," says Roy Heenan. "That's what it is, and it's short on facts. I am frankly horrified to hear the Human Rights Commission slander a Bell Canada supervisor with no facts upon which to base it. That may be an acceptable position for Mrs. Dainton to take, but it certainly is not an acceptable position for the Canadian Human Rights Commission. What facts have you heard to allow such slander? I repeat, I am *horrified* in the name of Mr. Restivo.

"What's more," he continues, "the Commission's *own investigator* found there was no substance to Mrs. Dainton's complaint, and his report recommended dismissal. I say this to point out that an impartial person came to totally different conclusions with the same information. My friend suggests that these investigators go around putting the parties to considerable trouble to amass all this, so that the Commission can then ignore it. If the Commission is to act fairly, it must act on the information which its investigator has put before it."

He reads some gobbledygook, and then translates. "The Commission has a duty to represent the public interest, not a private interest, not the complainant Mrs. Dainton in general. I would find it equally repugnant for the Canadian Human Rights Commission to represent both itself and an employer. I don't think it's proper for them to take a position which is so obviously one-sided. This is particularly objectionable given that their investigator's report recommended the rejection of Mrs. Dainton's complaint. I am equally disturbed when I hear there was a successful complaint against Bell in 1972, because I'm not aware of it."

"I have the document.," Eberts interjects. "The complaint was resolved without a hearing."

"Then in our view, it was abandoned," says Heenan. "It was unsuccessful. To be told it was successful makes a mockery of any notion of fairness. I also know Mrs. Dainton has made other complaints to the Human Rights Commission, not against Bell but against real estate brokers and dealers. I did not know that at the time of investigation."

I didn't know this either but understand that he's calling her *vexatious*. An activist. A busybody. Someone who can't be taken seriously.

"Surely these matters are irrelevant," Eberts cuts in again.

"Bell's position is simple," continues Heenan, unruffled by the interruption. "Mrs. Dainton was a good employee when she was with Bell. The suggestion that the company tried to get rid of her is nonsense. The suggestion that Mr. Restivo had something against Mrs. Dainton is nonsense, even to Mrs. Dainton's own knowledge. Since the time she left, Bell went through a radical change brought about by the regulators, which declared that Bell no longer had a monopoly, that other people could sell telephones and compete with Bell. And competition is fierce. You may have seen that little cartoon, *You don't like our telephone, try somebody else*. Well, there used to be nobody else and therefore selling a telephone was not difficult. But later, Bell realized it needed some aggressive, trained salespeople to compete against aggressive competition.

"In view of the fact that Mrs. Dainton indicated she wasn't interested in the sales job – that her interest was merely in using that to get into Bell to do three or four other jobs – they decided she was not really who they were looking for. I listened with great interest to my friend to try to find out where this *discrimination* was coming from. If I don't get a job, in my case maybe it's because I was born in Mexico, because I'm white, because I'm a lawyer. If I throw all those at you, you're going to say: *Now just a second, Mr. Heenan. What are you talking about?* In terms of the re-hiring, the only complaint I hear is *They didn't hire me,* and I just don't accept the leap to *therefore it must be.* You can't just throw a whole lot of epithets and say *this, this, this, this, and this.* Once you start throwing a potpourri of things…well, you'll notice the only thing that wasn't marked eventually was physical handicap or conviction with pardon.

"And then my friend says she sees no incompatibility between sex and race, and that she equates sex with family status – a nice trick, to be honest with you. Racial discrimination is well known. We certainly work hard against it at Bell, but the defences are entirely different."

"Mr. Heenan is suggesting that each ground should be a watertight compartment," interrupts Eberts. "You're either going on race, or sex, or family status. But it's widely accepted in the literature that there is a concept called *double disadvantage*, and that the grounds can be cumulative."

"Thank you," says the Chairman, shifting in his chair and adjusting his spectacles. "Ms. Eberts, on the question of conflict?"

"To the extent that my friend is suggesting that the Commission is bound by the investigator's report," Eberts begins, "I would counter that the proposition is simply wrong in law. The Commission has the discretion to come to its own independent decision. The Commission is not the arbiter of this complaint. *You* are."

She gestures towards the Chairman of the Tribunal with an impossibly precise flick of the eyebrows.

"My friend Mr. Heenan is suggesting that Mrs. Dainton should shoulder the cost of furthering the complaint before you. That would go against the long tradition of the Human Rights Commission. We should not force private individuals like Mrs. Dainton to fight human rights cases against large corporations like Bell. In this case, an important public issue must be advanced – *what is discrimination* and *how does this legislation function*? It will be valuable to the public to have the grounding of the Human Rights Code adjudicated upon."

"I don't attach a lot of weight to the question of who will fund each party," says the Chairman. "There are other methods of funding these proceedings."

"Legal aid?" says Eberts. "It doesn't apply, I'm sorry."

"The difficulty I have is this," interjects Heenan. "If the Commission is representing the public interest, it cannot ally itself with one party and blast a Bell Canada supervisor. What about *his* human rights? Who is protecting them and where is the public interest where Mr. Restivo is concerned? It's a violation of *his* human rights. Can the Commission get up and slander anyone in this room and then say it's in the public interest? If that's the public interest, I want no part of it."

"There is an incompatibility there," he continues, warming to his theme, "and it is fundamentally unfair for the Human Rights Commission to bias themselves by taking this position. They admit that at least some independent people *in their own employ* disagree with them. They can't decide the public interest is Mrs. Dainton against that nasty old Mr. Restivo and that miserable old Bell. Because I say: *Well, just a sec, where is the fairness?* What would Mrs. Dainton say if Ms. Eberts were here representing both Bell Canada and the Human Rights Commission? Mrs. Dainton would say: *Hey, that's unfair.*"

"I have been fairly patient but I'm out of patience now," Eberts snaps. "This really is not reply – it is repeat argument."

"I have to agree with you, Ms. Eberts," says the Chairman. "We're covering territory we've already covered. I believe all the complaints should be heard together, in that they arise from the same transaction between the Complainant and Respondent. I also believe the discretion of the Commission was exercised fairly. I'm not convinced the Commission has placed the private interest of the Complainant in conflict with the public interest."

The bell rings. I hand the first round to Eberts.

# 56. TACTICS AND DELAYS

Heenan betrays no sign of frustration. He glances at his opposing counsel, then directs his attention back to the Tribunal bench. Jumps to his feet again.

"Three matters were raised this morning which have never been raised before," says Heenan, displaying three fingers as arithmetic proof. "First is the 1972 complaint. Second is the allegation of some sort of prejudice by Mr. Restivo on account of an interracial marriage. Third is that the company allegedly wanted to rid itself of Mrs. Dainton in 1980.

"Now, Mr. Chairman, I have this great difficulty." That vague smile returns, detectable at the corners of his mouth, as if he is engaged in pitched battle against smugness. "These matters are not treated lightly. They are handled by an impartial investigator who is a lawyer – legal counsel for the Commission to ensure everything has been properly done – and that's why this is one of those things that takes *four years*.

"So, I must regretfully state that I will be obliged to go to the Federal Court to ask for a judicial review. It is a duty under the Human Rights Act to represent the public interest and I elevate that higher than just ensuring you have no conflict. The Commission cannot just throw the apparatus of the state against any person, whether private or corporate, on a mere whim, irresponsibly, unreasonably. Not when there is such a tremendous cost and effort involved in doing so.

"My friend has told us that she is going to bring in expert witnesses, although I was surprised it's even possible to get into expertise on the nature of the case as I understand it. But consider that there are reputations of other individuals and corporations at stake, and they find themselves being tarnished. There are allegations against Mr. Restivo which are quite serious. We question why there was even an investigation if it's just going to be, *Well, let's go and let the accused wander around in the darkness trying to figure out what the devil is happening*. Thank goodness we haven't adopted that procedure in law. These are not mere technical issues; they are fundamental. And for those reasons, Mr. Chairman, I would ask to adjourn these proceedings."

"Ms. Eberts?" says the Chairman after a short pause.

"Thank you." Eberts seems exhausted, taking her time to climb to her feet again and collect her thoughts.

"What my friend is complaining about in many respects is that he is a Respondent in a Human Rights proceeding. His complaints about Mr. Restivo being the target of my submissions this morning – why, they're nothing more than an allegation that the Human Rights Commission must not say naughty things about people who are Respondents in Human Rights proceedings. That is tantamount to saying that the Human Rights Commission must be a sort of toothless *amicus curia* before the Tribunal. And that, of course, is absurd."

An *amicus curia*, from its Latin origins, is a friend of the court who assists by offering impartial insight and expertise to a party that lacks adequate legal counsel. I can't help but imagine one as a mascot, an oversized tabby cat in spectacles, sitting next to my mother with arms folded stubbornly across its chest. I can't explain this image, nor explain this dream.

"My friend was aware of this Tribunal as soon as anyone else," Eberts continues, "and if he wanted to challenge the fact that the Commission rejected its investigator's report, he had weeks to apply for judicial review. This only serves to exercise the long purse of Bell Canada and delay this matter for another several months or years. This complaint was submitted in 1983, and five years have now elapsed. These are nothing more than bombastic tactics to get himself into Federal Court with a collection of allegations that go against the spirit and practice of human rights law in this country for the last forty years. By the time he finishes and is sent back to this hearing, three-quarters of the witnesses will be dispersed or dead. Allowing him to go to Federal Court on these spurious grounds would be absurd."

No sooner has Eberts dropped herself back in her seat than Heenan has already risen from his, as if bouncing from the opposite end of a playground see-saw. He's energized.

"Now, one of the most laughable statements made by my friend is that I'm asking for delays," says Heenan impishly, his campaign against smugness routed and in full retreat. "The delay of four years during the investigation is attributable to the Commission, not to Bell. She says I've known about this for some time, and that is not true. I was surprised. But it's not a question of surprise. It's a question of *fundamental fairness* that the accused party knows what case it is supposed to meet so that it is not tried by ambush. My friend Ms. Eberts told me this morning what her case was and it's entirely different from the one the Commission investigated. There's even a previous file at the Human Rights Commission which she is planning to present before you. Is that what my friend considers fairness?

"And to say these are *tactics and delays*," he scoffs, "I find equally amazing because Mrs. Dainton is now working, is no longer seeking employment, is instead looking for damages, and all those matters can be cured by money. Against that, you weigh the prospect of embarking on a confused, unfair, and costly proceeding which will consume a great deal of everybody's time."

He stops speaking without breaking eye contact with the Chairman.

"What I'm trying to clarify," drawls the Chairman, "is what this adjournment is for, so that I can clearly understand what is to transpire during that adjournment."

"The adjournment is to ask the Federal Court to prohibit the Human Rights Commission from playing the role they are attempting to play," responds Heenan without hesitation, "which is one in which they represent both interests. You said you didn't have any jurisdiction to deal with this and I think you're quite correct. In other words, Mr. Chairman, I can be *helpful*. I'm not trying to be difficult."

"Any further comments, Ms. Eberts?" asks the Chairman.

"Only to point out the danger in granting an open-ended adjournment, because there is no guarantee he will then be expeditious in his application to the Federal Court."

"I'd give him the benefit of the doubt, frankly," says the Chairman.

Mary Eberts makes one final plea.

"But even if there were any unfairness to him," she says, "it was cured this morning when he heard my opening remarks. He would remain in a fine position to prepare his case should he carry on with only a small adjournment."

When she sits down, the Chairman announces a brief recess and retreats to his chambers. A commotion of general chatter and movement erupts after he exits, along with huddles around both counsel tables. After a few minutes, the Chairman ambles back to the bench, taking a moment to shuffle into his seat and collect his thoughts.

"In my opinion," says the Chairman, "it behoves this Tribunal to deal with the substantive matters and once those are settled, the Respondent will be at liberty to have those decisions reviewed and either confirmed or overturned. This Tribunal will proceed to deal with the case before it."

I *feel* the hush fall over the room, as if the entire congregation has exhaled, and the mood lifts in the space occupied by Mary Eberts. The storm has abated, the sun emerges from the clouds, and the simple village folk descend from their homes.

Eberts nods. Heenan does not.

"It seems elementary under the Charter," says Heenan, half-standing and mounting his arms over the counsel table, "that a person who stands accused must know the grounds of the charge with precision. It becomes difficult for counsel to defend without knowing the elements and limits of the charges. So, I must respectfully except from this decision."

"That's your prerogative," says the Chairman.

"It's a fishing expedition!" explodes Heenan. His smile

has evaporated. "I don't even know now which complaint it is that we're proceeding on! I'm not going to walk out of here because I don't think that's the proper tack for counsel to take, and out of respect for you, sir. But I feel the public interest being meshed with the private interest puts me at a tremendous disadvantage. I can't even tell you what witnesses I'm going to call because it depends on whatever case this learned counsel can develop during these hearings, and which I will eventually have to meet. Nonetheless, I shall do my best to be as cooperative as I can with the Tribunal."

Beside him, Dace lowers her head. She cracks wide the jaws of her black briefcase and parcels the scattered documents scattered into neat stacks. Beside Mary Eberts, Audrey Macklin does the same.

And then, as if being vacuumed into the velvet void of that very briefcase, the fantasia ends and my world fades to black.

## 57. WHITESPLAINING

My mother isn't sleeping well, so I've brought her some pharmaceutical relief. I worry when she tells me she's not sleeping, because it reminds me of the elderly, pyjama-clad women I occasionally see in the emergency room, tortured by anxiety or insomnia, clinging to some trivial medical complaint to justify their visit, before eventually being discharged to putter around a lonely bungalow.

Sure enough, when I see her, my mother looks tired, moving slower than usual when she greets me at the door. She wears her mask to hug me, peels it off immediately, then retreats down the hallway with the lethargy of a goldfish swimming through an aquarium.

I've also brought back half of her court transcripts, possibly a different sort of intervention for insomnia. We head downstairs to the basement to file them away, my mother leaning on the banister for support.

"Would you march for Black Lives Matter now?" my mother asks as she accepts the folder from me. She doesn't wait for an answer because it's not a question but rather a triumphant statement. "Reading that transcript brings back those old feelings in me. If I were your age, I'd be right there in the crowds, marching alongside the protesters. But I'm almost seventy-eight years old now. I'm an *old lady*."

I shake my head. I'm not someone who marches.

My black side wants to be her acolyte, but Heenan's melodramatic indignation has spent the week ricocheting around my skull, made me disagreeable. *They didn't hire me, and I just don't accept the leap to therefore it must be*. My white half wonders, with dramatic reluctance, whether her legal case is airtight. My white half wants to ask her how racism can be a diagnosis of exclusion, and what that would mean for justice in the world.

"Bell dug their feet in," says my mother as she opens the antique suitcase again. "Christopher, there's so much paper there. How *dare* they when they saw what my record was."

"Doesn't it show how hard racism is to prove?" I say with trepidation. "There's no video, anywhere, of Bill Restivo with his knee on your neck."

"What do you mean *hard to prove*? It was open and shut!" She shuts the suitcase. "They knew they had an overqualified person who had worked for them like a dog for eleven years.

My friends called and told me they were hiring people from *off the street*."

"They lined up a lot of excuses," I point out, counting out three of them on my fingers. "That they were only hiring internally, that you were gunning for a different position than the one they were interviewing you for, that they wanted people with previous competitive sales experience…"

"Mmmhmm," hums my mother. "Then what about Mary Saunders? She was on my team, and they hired her back a year or two later, no questions asked. Just made a couple phone calls and she was back in. How do you explain that away?"

She swivels to face me.

"You've experienced it too in your life! You don't want to admit it. You just make excuses for things that should be obvious to anyone with eyes in their head."

I shake my head and look away. "I think sometimes you distort things through this lens of racism from a world that doesn't exist anymore. You want me to believe people see me differently because of my colour, and that's not true anymore. Even if it *were* true, it's not helpful to obsess over it."

"There you go, minimizing it again," she says, "never wanting to believe anybody is racist. And all around you, people are waking up. *We don't need Black faces who are not Black voices*, that's what they say now. And you don't want to acknowledge your own experiences. Next, you'll tell me you don't remember how they divided up the students in your high school by race."

This breaks the tension and catches me by surprise.

"What?"

"You don't remember having that conversation with me?"

"Which conversation?"

"Ah!" she exclaims. "When they'd do group projects at your high school, they would divide the students into racial groups. The white ones *here*, the Black ones *there*, the Indian ones *there*. You don't remember that conversation?"

"Who told you that?"

"Other parents told me. I…"

"I don't think that's even legal!" I protest.

"…Christopher, don't you remember? Whenever they had a school project, they would divide you up. I don't know if it was the teachers or the students who instigated it. But they would divide you up by *race*."

My exasperation boils over. My classmates certainly formed homogenous racial groups, as if magnetized, but my mother has confused it with modern apartheid. I might have unwittingly planted the seeds of this yarn decades ago – but from there, it has turned vine, with tentacles of imagined racism creeping in and choking all nuance.

I protest again.

"Mom, kids are cliquish, but you're confusing my high school with South Africa."

"But other parents said this too." She doubles down with absolute confidence. "I told you to get ready for it. And you told me you were *mixed*, so you would refuse to join any group. You said you'd wait until they called for the mixed children. You don't remember saying that?"

"No.".

"Christopher, you forget so much."

"I didn't forget it. It never happened."

Proof, if it were necessary, that memories can be twisted and corrupted by time. That lived experience never guarantees truth, nor does anything else.

"But this was the rumour," my mother trails off, with a thousand-mile stare. We start back up the staircase, returning to the living room, where my mother drops into her most comfortable chair. "The teachers loved you. It was the kids who were racist. You want to forget about them, how they were mad that you topped the class in everything."

"What makes you think they were racist?"

"The insults they would use. *Go back where you came from. Go back to the ghetto. Go pick some cotton.*"

My frustration swells again. More grains of truth that misrepresent my reality. I want to protest that I had every privilege growing up in this leafy suburb: a stable home and family, three round meals a day. I poached Black scholarships away from more convincingly disadvantaged minorities. My world was never smaller because of my race. If anything, I was a parasite, pocketing the advantages of plausible Blackness and giving nothing back.

"They were just *kids*," I instead retort. "Kids pick the lowest hanging fruit. If you're overweight, they'll call you fat. If you have acne, they'll call you *pizzaface*. If your nose is too big, they'll call you ugly. And if you're Black, they'll tell you to go back to the ghetto."

In response, my mother sucks her teeth.

## 58. THE GREATEST PROJECT THAT EVER WAS OR WILL BE

"You know what comes to mind when I think of injustice?"

"What?"

"I think of Ms. Kozmin – the mousy one with the gigantic glasses, like she was looking out through two Coke bottles. My independent study project in grade twelve English. Everyone got excited about doing a standout ISP project."

"The magazine?"

"Mine was the fake Maclean's magazine," I confirm. "A thirty-page feature issue with half a dozen essays about cross-cultural visions of the apocalypse, fake advertisements between all the articles, all hand illustrated in full colour. I slaved over that magazine for months. Probably the best student project she ever got in her career."

How could it not be? That's what I was gunning for – *the ISP project to end all ISP projects*. I wanted her to retire still waiting for another student to put that kind of effort into one of her assignments.

"Then, when we got our grades back, she had subtracted seven percent because I hadn't *shown all my draft work.*"

"Still ninety-three percent, Christopher."

"And another girl in that same class had written an essay about modern feminism – just a regular four-page essay, like any other essay. She gave that girl *a hundred percent.* Even made a special morning announcement on the PA system congratulating her by name."

My mother feigns polite surprise, but only because she might not remember just *how spectacular* that magazine had been. How shamelessly, euphorically over the top.

"I walked into that classroom after hours – her best student, all meek and shy – and Ms. Kozmin was sitting alone at her desk with the lights off, doing whatever it is teachers do after class is over. And I dropped that laminated Maclean's magazine on the desk in front of her. I stood there and told her the grade was an insult to the amount of work I put in. Asked her how she could justify it. Can't tell you if she was motivated by racial bias."

"Mmmhmm. She had her *knee on your neck.*"

"No. It never crossed my mind, but even if there were a chance it was racism, it wouldn't matter. I would never have wanted to allow her that indignation. I'd never want to leave her with the slightest opportunity to feel like she was the victim and not me. To pretend like *she* had been injured by an unfair accusation of bigotry."

"And what happened in the end?"

"She added four percent."

## 59. SNAKES AND LADDERS

In the standard configuration of *Snakes and Ladders*, the longest snake is the one whose head sits on the gameboard's eighty-seventh space.

It slides the unlucky victim all the way back down to the twenty-fourth space, making it also the point in gameplay when the board is most likely to be overturned, with all players in agreement that it's time to run around outdoors.

But nowadays, amid this pandemic lockdown, the outdoors no longer exists. Only this pile of manila envelopes and those piles of grey cloud outside my window. From this point forward, the substance and merit of my mother's human rights case never surface again. Instead, in July 1989, Roy Heenan asks the Federal Court for something called a *Prohibition order*, which appears to be a fashionable boot designed to squash the earlier decision to appoint a Human Rights Tribunal in the first place.

The law is both tortuous and torturous. Heenan argues that the Commission arrived at their initial decision by relying on *unfair grounds* (the old successful complaint against Bell and the personal animus towards my mother of the now-infamous Bill Restivo). What's more, Heenan suggests that the Commission relied upon Bart Sackrule's confidential report both without Bell Canada's consent, and without giving Bell the chance to comment on it. Tortuous, yes, but both actions are expressly prohibited by the Human Rights Act, so not to undermine what is supposed to be a confidential settlement process.

In other words, the Commission broke the rules of *natural justice*. Torturous.

Roy Heenan is a busy man, so a year later, he becomes the one irritated by tactics and delays.

"My question is simple," he writes. "Does the Commission wish to settle this matter or not? Let's get on with it."

He knows he has his adversary on the ropes on technical grounds. To drive his point home, he attaches ten additional letters to his own, including a grovelling letter from the Commission pleading that my mother should consent to any settlement. A short time later, the Commission concedes, and Bell files another baffling legal document known as a *Notice of Discontinuance*.

Shortly afterwards, Mary Eberts reviews the file and writes an eloquent 18-page autopsy of the case. The Human Rights Commission's Rene Duval studies her report and decides to have my mother's file independently re-assessed by a law professor. He's wondering if this corpse can be somehow resurrected.

By March, that law professor agrees the Commission made an innocent mistake on the eighty-seventh space of the gameboard. He suggests sending this case of prejudice back to the ground floor to be re-evaluated without prejudice. Snakes and ladders.

And finally, in October 1991 – fully eight years after her original complaint – my mother receives a letter from the Commission, this one from someone named Sidney Lederman. He says he can't appoint a new Tribunal until the

Commission makes a formal request sometime this month, probably around the twenty-fourth space.

He'll let her know.

Sit tight.

## 60. FRUIT FLIES LIKE A BANANA

That's it. There's no more.

I rummage through dog-eared documents and torn envelopes spread over the kitchen island. There's no follow up letter to be found, so I pick up the phone and call the Commission myself.

"If the case if over ten years old, we would have destroyed the files," a voice named Rosalie explains. "The Commission doesn't retain records beyond 2010."

"So, is there any way to reopen the case file? Because to my knowledge, the case was never resolved."

"We can only accept new complaints that occurred within the last year," says Rosalie.

"But this is an old complaint."

"The Commission can't revisit old complaints."

"If you've destroyed all the records of the old complaint, then I suppose that would make it a new complaint."

"We can only accept new complaints that occurred within the last year."

Checkmate.

Frustrated and demoralized, I set my phone down, push aside the pile of torn envelopes, and pick up my mother's university essay, that forbidden artifact that lobs out obsolete words like *negro* and *mongoloid*. Each anachronism stings my eyes like a papercut under a faucet. On and on about how the British held themselves aloof from the darker peoples, leaving the most favoured positions for mulattoes like me. The whiter the skin, the greater the dominance. *Yellow, black, or red skin mean hereditary submission, subordination, and inferiority.* All justified by the white man's burden, whereby whites reluctantly bowed to their destiny to rule over lesser breeds.

Heavy stuff. But maybe somewhere in here, the past has something to say about the present.

But before it does, my mother tackles the changing place

of what she refers to as the *backward negro* relative to *the white man*. For two and a half centuries, slavery was that place, but even slavery was always changing. The slavery of 1850 hardly resembled the slavery of 1650. Since abolition, the negro-white relationship has continued to change, and *never more rapidly than now*. Competition for jobs. Neighbourhoods filled with people whose appearance and speech seem strange. The status quo threatened. An outgroup, she says, becomes an object of hatred or violent rejection when it threatens the comfort or security of the in-group. A reaction sets in.

> Many have seen with their own eyes that negroes are all too commonly dirty, diseased, uneducated, irresponsible, and otherwise lacking in those qualities that the white man likes to apply exclusively to his own race.

I bristle at this inventory of our presumed faults. *Don't think about elephants* predictably conjures up the mental image of a leathery, hooved beast trundling across the savannah, and my mother's words conjure up the most primitive Black stereotypes. Quite a trick.

*Is the negro inferior to the white man?* My mother's casual use of third person, male gendered language is jarring. She's blunt: she's asking the tough questions. The white man assumes Black behaviour is born of race and biology, when it instead reflects his social caste. In the civil rights era, the first compromise was the birth of *the Southern darky*, according to my mother. I glimpse those words ahead of me, and my fascinated eyes scour the surrounding passage.

> As a subordinate, the negro is comparatively safe from aggression by the white man. Superior in every respect, the white man has no strong urge to put the negro in his place. The role of the conventional Southern darky is a part the negro has learned to play because it has been ascribed to him, part of an elaborate caste society, reflected in the personality of the negro.

But it's a role nobody cares to play anymore. Friction happens when modern negroes like Viola Desmond no longer accept discourtesies and provocations without retaliation.

It's hard to imagine what feelings the Prince Edward Island locals harboured around her. Curiosity of the comfortable sort in which their dominance was never was in jeopardy. With no experience of Black folks, the Reverend's only knowledge presumably came from books – until one lone Black student submitted this vaguely threatening essay for his appraisal. She wants him to project himself into the world of the negro and learn *the depressing effects of frustration, embarrassment, and deprivation.* Much distortion and confusion exist concerning the wants of the negro, she says, and because of this, bitterness is sharpened, and fears are imagined.

# 61. GUILTY WHITE MEN

I turn the page and burrow deeper into what has become a revolutionary manifesto disguised as a sociology term paper. This faceless, featureless *white man* has a lot to atone for. An uncomfortable read for the Reverend, one such guilty white man.

I hope he didn't take it personally. My mother never meant to be dramatic, and without intent, words are just noises. *Time flies like an arrow; fruit flies like a banana.* Language has evolved, barely a generation later. Her intent is unchanged, but her words are dusty antiques.

> Most people are not naturally reflective any more than naturally malicious, and the white man keeps the black man at a certain remove to avoid being called to account for the crimes of his forefathers.

My eyes linger on this innocuous passage, my white side bothered by it more than by the liberal use of *negro*, *mulatto*, and *darky*.

Punishing sons and daughters for the sins of their forefathers sounds antithetical to justice. *The son shall not suffer for the iniquity of the father,* claims the Old Testament. *The righteousness of the righteous shall be upon himself, and the wickedness of the wicked shall be upon himself.*

Now, I'm not so sure. I can't square those lofty principles with righting the wrongs of Bell, Dace Phillips, and Roy Heenan – one a corporation, two now dead – and of Bill Restivo, who must now be as old as my mother. Ma Bell is the malevolent parent, and my mother came looking for the kind of justice found elsewhere in the Old Testament: *he will by no means leave the guilty unpunished, visiting the iniquity of fathers on the children and on the grandchildren to the third and fourth generations.*

But then, out of nowhere, maybe there's still hope.

We must learn the problems of the white man, both real and imagined, his misgivings, his prejudices, his fears. These cannot be sneered into non-existence. The emotional impact of a lifetime of subconscious indoctrination cannot be ignored just because it shouldn't be there. For a white man, these are real problems, and if there is to be a solution, these problems must be approached realistically.

*Finally*, the Reverend must have thought, alone in his office with only his prejudices for company. *Finally, someone cares about my fears and misgivings as a white man.*

This must have been the precise moment when the Reverend chose to award my mother an 'A'.

Smart man.

Good.

## 62. WAR PROFITEERING

This is not a good table.

It might be strategically positioned next to the café window, but it has one short leg, so it wobbles when I rest my elbows. It wobbles again when Jessica rests her elbows on the other side. When I release my weight, the wobbly table springs back, jolting my paper cup. Its contents splash up and over the rim, dripping down the near side and creating an untidy puddle that soaks into the napkin.

"Okay, here's the problem," I say, leaning in to sip espresso from the soggy cup. "You have one group with these noble ideas: due process, evidence, justice. Let's call them *white people*. And you have this opposing group with all these subjective negative experiences. They're all piled up like cordwood, those experiences. And so, there's this undercurrent of perceived injustice and frustration, just like...just like this table with the short leg. Just a constant irritation. And the first group says to the second one, *okay, if we've wronged you so bad, then show us the proof*, but the second group always comes back emptyhanded. Because it's *hard*, right?"

"Right."

"So, someone wads up some paper and kicks it under the short leg, and you test it out, you put your elbow on it. And the table still wobbles, but now it wobbles in a different direction. And eventually, the whole table thing becomes this endless distraction, and before you know it your drink is stone cold."

"Right. Okay, so it's like a metaphorical table. Which way is the metaphorical table leaning now?"

"I can't say for sure, but if you want to know what the cultural *zeitgeist* is, just try saying the opposite out loud."

What I imply, but don't dare say out loud, is that the social justice cult is ascendant. Challenge its maxims and you'll be tarred and feathered in the town square. But even if *anti-racism* is dominant, it still styles itself the underdog. A countercultural force. I recline in my seat, satisfied with how clever I've been. The table recoils, spilling Jessica's tea.

"I dunno," I add. "Maybe eventually you need a whole new table."

"What, like apartheid?"

"No, not apartheid." My metaphor has reached its limits. "All I know is my parents raised to be one of those *process* people, so I didn't really get the second group – the one out there stewing over their *experiences*. But now, my mom wants to indoctrinate me with all those social justice things we're supposed to believe now. She wants me to date someone who understands the *mixed experience*. But then again, she married a white man, not a Black man, and that's why I'm here in the first place."

"Ironic, isn't it?"

"No, she hates irony. She finds it unpleasant."

My eyes glaze, and my thoughts briefly dissolve into the rumbling chatter of the café, the clatter of distant cups, and the whirr of the espresso machines.

"So now, that second group is jamming as many wads of paper as it can under that table leg. And I'm just paralysed. I mean, what's the statute of limitations on this human rights case? Is it even fair for people who *weren't* responsible to pay for the actions of those who *were*? And, like, what did I ever do that deserves compensation in the first place? Some people bilk an inheritance out of their elderly parents, and here I am taking advantage of my mother being jerked around by Bell Canada for a decade."

Jessica laughs. "What child ever deserved to inherit a dime? It's their *birth right*, just try telling them any different.

Don't act like this is the end of history or something. This can of worms is nothing new."

I nod. She continues. "The Chinese believe in this three-lifetime rule. Karmic beliefs anyway. If you fucked up, your future generations pay for it in their own way for exactly three generations. Health issues, birth defects. And then, *kaput*. Done."

"How very Old Testament."

She sips her tea. "Everyone should study Chinese folk religions and Confucianism. I mean, these people have been around for thousands and thousands of years, and their civilization is still around, intact. It's vanity to think you're above a three-thousand-year-old civilization.

"Besides, we already send plenty of money to the First Nations," she continues. "Not enough, but enough so we all feel better. So, Bell should at least do the same. Give them a chance to be part of something larger than themselves, and they'll feel better too. Why can't you be on the winning team for once?"

# 63. FOOD FOR THOUGHT

Here it is. An entire online calendar devoted to protests in support of the *status quo*.

I frown. It's strange to march in defence of the *status quo*, but my mother would celebrate it. No matter that the new consensus already positions equity, diversity, and inclusion as the sacred cows of the modern office – just another of the well-meaning ways the corporate world has evolved since 1983. I'm already convinced, but I text my thoughts anyway to the male-bonding chat group we playfully call *No Ma'am*, which consists of Matt, a white high school vice-principal; Mike, a white corporate negotiator; and Nick, an Indian office executive.

When I claim that only grassroots community activism will keep diversity, equity, and inclusion on the 2020 agenda, I'm being ironic. It's a subtle rebellion that my mother wouldn't understand this. She reviles all flavours of irony and cynicism, even though I find them cathartic.

Matt responds by directing me to his school board's equity, diversity, and inclusion website.

> Welcome to THE ARK, a Toronto Catholic District School Board website for equity, diversity, and inclusion. From the story of Noah, THE ARK reminds us of God's prophetic call to change our ways of thinking and living. We journey together in self-reflection on our own biases (40 days) and in solidarity through a difficult transformation (flood). As we dismantle the systems of oppression, let us move towards peace (dove), healing (olive branch), and community of hope and love (rainbow).

"How many days into your self-reflection are you?" I ask after scanning the contents of the page.

"There's never a day when I stop reflecting. In fact, I'm looking in the mirror right now, and I plan on reciting that paragraph word for word when I interview for principal," he responds, adding a dash of verbal irony.

"You're the wrong colour to be principal," I point out ironically, "If you're serious about the job, I'd recommend showing up to the interview in blackface."

"A guy did that a few years ago," says Matt. "He's Prime Minister now."

"That Noah's Ark analogy is high irony," Mike interjects.

Another powerful and successful white man. "Think about it: the basic social justice narrative they're trying to support is illogical, but it *must* be accepted as dogma. It has a mythic quality that requires faith, just like religious stories."

"Strange story to choose considering the flood is all about a vengeful God set on destroying the world," says Matt, allowing the situational irony to tickle his taste buds. These white men and their ideas.

Ellipses in the chat. Nick, an Indian and model minority, has evidently begun to type something, before he reconsiders and allows the white men to continue.

"Even they see the parallels, albeit without self-awareness," continues Mike. "*Appease and atone or an angry God will punish us.*"

"Who said anything should be logical these days?" says Matt.

"So now you get what I'm saying," I conclude. "As long as nothing makes perfect sense, I might as well join the winning team."

Again, I can't explain any of this to my mother, who hates irony. I can't explain that I'm torn, convinced something unfair happened to her forty years ago, but equally convinced the same injustice could never happen today. That I'm equally conflicted over what the consequences to this amorphous corporation should be. Maybe I should just switch my mobile service to Rogers.

Here's the problem: boomers are the generation of the cat clinging to a clothesline, caption reading *Hang in there, baby*. They gravitate to the literal, and my mother can barely handle surface irony: *lovely weather today* but it's snowing, *Nothing is written in stone*, carved into a cliff face. Irony: a situation contrary to what's expected. The expression of meaning with language that signifies the opposite. But surface irony to millennials is like Tylenol to a junkie. Millennials hide their intentions in multiple layers of code, the more confusing, the better. The earnest and the ironic eventually become hopelessly muddled, marking a miraculous return from irony to sincerity. *Post-irony* marks a return that is both absurd and completely sincere. Word of the day.

Like a five-dollar bill with my mother's face. Who says she hasn't been through the same adversity as Viola Desmond? That phony fiver is every bit as appropriate as Canada's very real ten-dollar bill. That's *post-irony*, but my mother would never want to hear about it. She hates irony.

Or maybe it's the wrong question. Maybe it doesn't even matter if the world has changed since Bell had its way. People need purpose and struggle. To be part of something big, even with poppies in bloom on yesterday's battlefields.

Maybe I'm out to prove the world is different. Mike would say none of it matters; that protest is all meaningless symbolism. I can't promise he's wrong. But protesting is still part of this narrative. March first. Believe later. That's *post-irony*.

# 64. BARONESS BELL'S PRISMATIC CORPORATE RESPONSIBILITY ACTUATOR

I start over.

First, I tear my original letter into half-inch strips, then tear those strips into confetti, which I sprinkle into the wastebasket. Then, I sit down at my computer and tap out a whole new letter to Bell Canada, addressing this one to Media Relations.

This time, I tell them I'm writing a book about the role of Bell in a case of covert racism involving my mother. I call them hypocrites when it comes to social injustice and offer them the chance to correct the record. I provoke them outright: maybe they'd like to reiterate Bell's position that while implicit racism probably exists somewhere, it couldn't have been a factor in depriving L. Dainton of her former sales position. Or more optimistically, maybe they'd prefer to acknowledge that Bell erred in a consequential way. If so, I humbly suggest that an apology and a charitable donation in my mother's name would be a form of restitution that would give this narrative a happier ending. Because I'm no race war profiteer.

I show the letter to Mike before hitting send. He's not impressed.

"A corporation isn't a villain," says Mike. "It's an entity with inputs and outputs, like one of those clanking diesel contraptions you find in Jules Verne novels, with all the cogs and sails and exhaust pipes. And all that Victorian steampunk machine is going to do here is calculate whether this letter can go in the round file."

He's right. I'm still fooling myself believing such a fantastical apparatus has any capacity for good, evil, or even hypocrisy. Like a toaster or a washing machine, it has neither memory nor conscience. My input is as likely to be chewed up by the rusted brass gears as to cause it to churn out anything meaningful.

And even if it did, it would still just be a clanking machine.

# 65. HISTORY, ART, AND OPPRESSION

I crouch with a two by four-foot white slab of foamboard laid out in front of me and the sounds of instrumental bossa nova playing through the speakers.

The poster board is lightweight but sturdy. I use a ruler and a stencil to outline the letters in pencil, then begin the tedious work of filling them in with blue marker. This project reminds me of high school, because back then, *every class* became arts and crafts at least part-time.

Our teachers insisted we create title pages for every new section of our notebooks – any excuse for a pop of colour between unrelenting text blocks of handwritten notes. Mine were never any good. My modest efforts were betrayed by my lack of artistic talent, although what Art had to do with History was never clear. My history teacher was a common ginger whose shock of orange hair crowned a pale and freckled face. More than white, he was *aggressively* white – like some sort of Viking special agent sent by time machine to infiltrate the modern world.

Enough daydreaming. Back to the task at hand. My foamboard is coming along in title page-like fashion: the word *RACISM* is the largest, but its last two letters are absurdly cramped. Artistic licence.

No better than that mediocre title page for my insignificant History notebook, which barely scored a passing grade. It was no Maclean's magazine, but nor was I used to scraping by with those types of marks. I was annoyed, but nowhere near as annoyed as my mother.

It was yet another example of how the world *holds Black children back*, she concluded, sensing a touch of Bill Restivo in this unfortunate Viking. A Black student's title page needed to be *twice as good* as the next one to make the same grade. No sooner had I shown her my score than she had diagnosed my History teacher with chronic white supremacy. With that, she marched into school on parent-teacher night, race card in hand, to insinuate he was a common bigot. *Bigotus vulgaris.*

She meant well, rising to my defence the way no one had for her, but I felt uncomfortable and ashamed. Telepathically convicting this redhead of *racism* seemed imprecise – and being imprecisely accused of something so vile was unfair. Maybe my title page just hadn't been very good.

"Sometimes your best isn't good enough," I suggested timidly. "Isn't that a better childhood lesson?"

No. Not to her.

"There are a lot of these people hidden in North America," she explained later. Hidden they certainly were – they'd have to be. But ferret them out she would, with the same enthusiasm of crackpot working his way up the beach with a metal detector.

I toss my marker aside and stand up. Stretch. Step back to inspect my work. My sign is confusing, silly, and amateurish, but legible. It will have to do.

I'm ready.

## 66. THE WRONG KIND OF ALLY

---

I've been hiding my sign on the walk over, holding it backwards and upside down. Despite this, passers-by still tilt their heads in shameless attempts to read the text. Halfway up Yonge Street, I pass a mailbox. Someone has scrawled across it in black marker:

DISARM TORONTO POLICE
DEFUND
ABOLISH

I frown. All of this feels suddenly too radical, and I wonder again if this is a good idea. Cynics don't march for social justice, and introverts don't march, full stop. My rational mind turns to walk home but my body and my legs don't follow.

This is a protest versus police brutality, and when I finally melt into the hip Queen Street crowd, I worry I'm holding the wrong kind of sign. Most of the slogans around me are variations on themes of *Black Lives Matter* or *I can't breathe*. Some protest the mistreatment of Indigenous Canadians at the hands of the police. Others call for prisons to be abolished. Others are vague. *Enough is enough* or *Silence is betrayal*. Mine is most confusing of all.

Our route will take us down the length of Queen Street and up University Avenue, before ending at the police station on Dundas Street, where the organizers have planned a short rally. What a strange feeling, being Black but not Black enough to be in this crowd, and never having protested in my life. I'm the wrong kind of ally, a fraud.

But even if I don't dare speak a whisper of cynicism, I've brought my own cause to fill that space. Even if I'm not sure whether all Black people deserve reparations for the horror of slavery, I can at least get behind the idea that, at a minimum, my mother deserves some.

We pass the graffiti alley, where flashes of spraypainted artwork peek through a labyrinth of brick facades, plywood-boarded windows, and derelict scaffolding. The alleys are normally home to an exuberant fusion of colourful caricatures, abstractions, and pop art, but they're now fully adorned with *Black Lives Matter* slogans and the meticulously rendered faces of Black revolutionaries and community organizers.

The atmosphere is festive by the time our congregation reaches the concrete barriers that gate the police precinct. Some protesters raise their arms to make their presence known, and others are jumping, the only way to stay warm in November. Most are younger than me, college age at best. Black coats, black tuques, black bags, black pants. Some march in black combat boots and army fatigues.

They clap as they chant.

I'm not chanting, and I can't clap because of the sign I'm holding.

BELL CANADA: DEAF TO RACISM

## 67. THE BLACK COLLECTIVE

It's a party. No question.

"What do we want?"

"JUSTICE!"

"When do we want it?"

"NOW!"

That's what they're shouting in their euphoria, faces flushed by the autumn chill, but I stay silent. My voice isn't one designed for shouting. Bystanders are inspecting my sign with confusion, and that's making me tense. My armpits are sweating.

A woman my age stands next to me, holding a sign. *My skin colour does not determine my worth,* it says in thick black Sharpie over a fluorescent orange background. Her poster matches her fluorescent orange jumpsuit, and clashes in spectacular fashion with the blue headwrap knotted like a cloth nipple over her forehead. Her skin isn't quite *Abagbe* Black, but she's certainly Black enough. One look and I decide I'd feel equally silly trading signs with her, so maybe I should get over myself.

When she sees me reading her sign, she edges closer. The chanting has stopped, for now, and she seizes the opportunity.

"I've never seen you at one of these before." An unmistakeably African accent over the rumble of the crowd. She smiles. "Welcome."

"Thank you." I smile back.

"Bell Canada." She looks at my sign thoughtfully.

"It's sort of my mother's thing," I apologize, and then hesitate. She waits, reasonably expecting more.

"I've never been out here…to one of these. I don't know how comfortable I feel with all this."

She continues facing me, inexplicably interested in my inexplicable sign.

"It's hard to make a case in ten words or less," I say, nodding towards my poster. Another bead of sweat tickles as it runs from my armpit to chest. "My mother came from Trinidad, worked hard her whole life."

I stop, worried the chants will resume, drown me out before I can complete my elevator pitch. Worried she'll lose interest. But she nods, egging me on. "Then Bell Canada refused to rehire her after she left for maternity leave, so she took them to the Human Rights Commission. That's it. So, this might be the wrong march, but I'm not sure what the right march is."

My voice cracks at the end. It's no good for noisy spaces. It's too loud for a debate here, and this sell job wasn't nearly enough.

"Mmmhmm," she hums. "No, this is the right march. Nobody is innocent. All of Canada is not innocent, and we need to resist the racism that is everywhere. When I came here, I went to nursing school in Kingston. Queen's University is so racist. All these institutions are."

That was too easy. "Came here from where?" I try to mirror her natural curiosity. "I went to school in Kingston too."

"Nigeria. People here have so many misconceptions about Nigeria. They talk about the email scams, and they think Nigeria is corrupt."

"But…it's not?" I'm rationing my words because this is no place to talk. As if on cue, the crowd erupts around us, as if the home team has just taken the field.

"Everywhere is equally corrupt, and everywhere has its problems. America is corrupt. Canada is corrupt. I would never point out the flaws in Nigeria, I will defend it to my death."

"And what's wrong with Queen's?"

She tries to answer me, but the Black woman with the megaphone has descended into a religious frenzy, leading a spirited call and response. This can't be her first mass. Her skill is in inspiring a crowd.

"If Black people don't get it?" the megaphone woman demands to know.

"SHUT IT DOWN!" My radical new companion

pumps her fist into the air in unison with the frenzied crowd. I stay silent.

"If Indigenous people don't get it?"

"SHUT! IT! DOWN!"

The Nigerian woman guides me by the shoulder, away from the woman with the megaphone, through a chaos of bodies and towards the sidewalk. Soon, the crowd thins out enough that I can hear her speak.

"People from Kingston don't even understand what Nigeria is," she begins again. "They tell me *your English is exceptionally good*, as if English is not already the common language in Nigeria."

I laugh uncomfortably. I know Kingston, Ontario, and it's asking a lot to expect small town folks to know the official languages of all fifty-four countries in Africa.

"Many of them consider Black people to be like animals. I remember one patient who said to me *I just don't like Black people* when I went into his room. My preceptor offered to take me off the assignment, but I decided to kill him with kindness instead."

"And did you…kill him in the end?"

She laughs.

I tell her I'm in medicine too, and that I was one of

only four Black medical students in my class. The year after I graduated, there was only one, and she was front page news. Later, I would do a year of residency in the same unfussy town she did her nursing degree. If there was racism to find, I was oblivious to it.

No problem, because racism is now a disability, I point out, straining not to invalidate her experience. What use is being personally racist when culture and institutions are aligned against you? For a shameless redneck nowadays, it's just hard to operate in polite company. Patients who direct their slurs towards nurses and paramedics, the ones who demand to see a doctor who isn't *foreign*, they're ostracized by their healthcare team. Pigment is now a lubricant, one that makes it easier to navigate today's world.

Once, I recall, a Black patient even thanked me for being one of the few Black doctors. *You're welcome*, I said, as if I had anything to do with it. As if being Black alone were somehow enough.

"When I would date," she continues, undeterred, "the men at Queen's would see me as exotic. One of them said to me, to my face, *I've never had a Black girl before.*"

"That's awkward."

"I went on another date with a white man and while we ate dinner, he told me *my grandpa is super racist, but you'll be fine*."

I nod. "That's saying the quiet part out loud."

None of this bothered my mother in Prince Edward Island, a place rural and white enough to make Kingston, Ontario resemble Lagos, Nigeria by comparison. Either this protester is more sensitive than my mother, or my mother was equally oblivious to the systemic oppression mobilized against her in the Maritimes. The same way I'm an oblivious fool.

"One preceptor told me I'd never be a nurse. She would say things to me that nobody would say to a white person. Another professor told me *You should try not being so aggressive* to explain why she gave me a poor grade on my clinical rotation. As if all Black women are aggressive."

I nod again. I'm not sure what to say, but I know a microaggression when I hear one. My empathy would be empty because I can't tell by looking at her whether she's a good nurse or a bad one – I just don't have enough information. Just like all drivers think they're excellent drivers, all doctors and nurses think they're excellent healthcare professionals. We can't all be right. It would be unfair to believe her unconditionally.

Patronizing.

"No wonder you have mixed feelings about Queen's," I conclude. I guess we're all just more fragile these days. The world has primed us to see injustice everywhere.

"My feelings are not *mixed*," she snaps. "Listen, there was one university project that I worked on with another girl who was *white*, and our papers were almost identical, but we earned two different marks. How else can you explain that?"

I can't. All I can do is take her word for it. If only we all carried hard evidence in our backpacks: my mother's Bell portfolio, my Maclean's magazine, her university project. But her vision of a world shrouded in racism doesn't inspire me. It's disempowering. Whatever truth it holds, my brain rejects it like uncooked meat.

"My mother loved her experience in Prince Edward Island," I say carefully. "She thought they were just a bunch of well-meaning, genuinely curious small-town people. It wasn't until she got to the big city that she felt like the world was out to get her."

That is, she was never a revolutionary until Bell forced her hand. My companion has no reason to believe me either, any more than I should believe her. But as I say this, it dawns that I believe it, perhaps for the first time, entirely unironically. Maybe my scepticism is as genetic and tribal as race or sexual orientation. All this time, I've been terrified that my hesitation would come across as racist. My armpits are moist with the fear of being cast out, shouted down, lynched by the radical mob surrounding me. But there was never any cause for worry.

My nameless companion beams at me. "I like this. Your mother would be happy that you are here."

I stand with her for several more minutes, then turn my sign upside down and retreat through this hive of Blackness, anonymous faces, chanting, and revolutionary energy. There's anger here, but also unity and celebration. I'm not fully one with that unity, but I'm about halfway to being on the winning team. It's a good start.

# 68. DEPARTMENT OF TACTICAL REGRET

"So, I took your advice."

I shiver with excitement because part of me thinks this is the triumph I've been waiting for. I sip my espresso and grin foolishly across the café table.

"Look at you, fighting and marching for justice," says Jessica. "You're like *Malcolm X*."

"Should I clear my calendar for a face-to-face with Mirco Bibic? Should I wear a tie? I don't know how my mother will feel about commuting downtown in the dead of winter for her in-person apology. She hates the snow."

I push the phone sideways across the table and let Jessica read the email herself, scrolling down as her eyes track the bottom of the screen.

> I lead the workplace practices team in Human Resources at Bell. I was sorry to read about your mother's experience. We appreciate the opportunity to respond and provide you with some information on our current initiatives.
>
> As I am sure you can appreciate, our files from that time are not readily accessible but we are gathering any information we may have. If you would like to have a call to provide additional context, I would be happy to do that – just let me know when would work for you.
>
> Jennifer

I take another sip.

"When I looked her up, turns out she's white and she's a lawyer. She was boss of legal services at the Nova Scotia Department of Justice, and now she's Vice-President of Total Rewards and Human Resources. She deals with mental health and disability. She's *somebody*."

Jessica takes a sip. "Everybody thinks they're somebody. That doesn't mean anything. Sounds like she just wants to tell you what they're up to, not arrange for reparations. But she still sounds sweet. I bet she's gorgeous. You should ask her out."

## 69. PACKING PEANUTS

Here we are. The climax.

Start to finish, the conversation takes fifteen minutes.

First, a glass of wine to steady my nerves, and then I dial the number at the bottom of the email. I ask if I caught her at a good time and thank her for graciously taking my call. I sound articulate and measured, like a mature doctor and not some crank with an axe to grind. God knows the world has enough of those.

Jennifer begins by building rapport. Puts me at ease asking what it's like being a frontline healthcare hero during a pandemic. I tell her the emergency department quiets down paradoxically just as community infections rise and that the true heroes are the friends we made along the way. Then we move to the substance.

She couldn't get any records, unfortunately, given how long ago all this happened. Any records from antiquity were ceremonially burned after ten years. This news, Jennifer murmurs, cushioning her words with soft layers of eloquent, top-shelf regret. Her voice is gentle, like a lullaby.

"I got in touch with the Human Rights Commission and reached the same impasse." It's my most professional voice. "All I have left is a basement littered with paper records. Piles and piles of letters and transcripts. When you're a kid, you don't really know what your parents went through."

Jennifer hadn't realized my mother had gone all the way to a Tribunal, nor that Bell had gone and hired Heenan Blaikie.

"That gives us some direction."

I'm not exactly sure which direction she means, except one that lets them trace the brand of shredder used to obliterate the records.

"On a technicality, they sent it back down to the Commission." I fill in the details. "And that's where the letters and records suddenly stop. My mom just didn't have the emotional bandwidth to keep fighting this thing."

It filled Jennifer with deep sadness to read my email and now, to hear first-hand about my mother's experience. She purrs the right social justice truisms and expresses her regret that Bell could have been so heartless, considering what model corporate citizens they are.

She conspicuously avoids disputing my claims. I should know Bell has made tremendous progress on workplace diversity since those days. She asks what happened to my mother afterwards and appreciates that she must be a *Very Strong Woman*.

"She became a French teacher," I say.

"Wonderful." It sounds sincere, but I wonder if her answer would have been similar had my mother ended up an accountant, a meth cook, or a carnie. It's not Jennifer's intent, surely, but her words suggest that everything turned out alright in the end.

I guess that's always true, in a cosmic sense.

"When I talk to her, she says that decade fighting Bell was the one thing that affected her most in her entire life."

More empathetic sounds from the other end of the line. It's like I'm rooting through the contents of a large cardboard box wrapped in Christmas paper, digging for the gift that must be buried somewhere at the bottom. But instead, the box is stuffed with Styrofoam packing peanuts. They're innumerable, light as cotton candy, and they cling to my hands and my clothes, and no matter how deep I plunge my hand, I only end up grasping at more peanuts.

"Something I struggle with," I continue with rising desperation, "is how to achieve a just resolution, especially since a corporation isn't a person. I mean, things that make sense from a human perspective don't really make sense from a corporate one."

"Mmm," says Jennifer.

"It's just strange to google *Bell Canada and racism* and find all these new initiatives. And then to contrast all that optimism and energy against my mother's treatment. Because thirty years ago, the same company took a reasonable person and systematically discredited her experience. How do you think it would play out differently if the same thing happened today?"

More sympathetic noises. She's calculated that it wouldn't be appropriate to explain the nuts and bolts of Bell's current workplace initiatives, so she settles for offering more packing peanuts. Nothing of substance. We have someone like this at the hospital too. A fixer. She handles patient complaints. She circles back, loops people in. Allows everyone to feel heard.

Makes them go away.

"Do you think she'd be open to talking with us?" Jennifer finally asks.

"I'd have to talk to her to know how she'd react," I say. "I'd have to think about how it would help her achieve closure given that you don't have any records and that there's some…information asymmetry. Interesting that there's no such thing as institutional memory. It's like the whole case has vanished without a trace."

I'd have to warn my mother about Jennifer's perfect fluency in the vacuous language of power: critical theory, anti-racism, poststructuralism, diversity, equity and inclusion. Warn her that Jennifer can bend and shape them to her will, like an agent in the *Matrix*. Warn her that Jennifer can wield words with such vehemence and sincerity that their delivery alone makes them true against all odds.

Later, Mike debriefs me on exactly what just happened.

"They don't care. This isn't how they make money," he says. "They want to give you a pat on the head and send you on your way. They couldn't give less of a shit."

## 70. PIE IN THE SKY

As I remove my coat in the hallway, I see with satisfaction that my mother has decorated the Christmas tree in the living room with dozens of ornaments, large and small, from her past teaching days. Nearly every branch is adorned with painted elves, fabric angels, ceramic polar bears, wooden sleighs, and plastic baubles with gold trim. She's scattered a few presents underneath the tree, and the banister leading upstairs is lined with faux evergreen wreaths.

"I talked to Jennifer," I begin, "and she was sorry to hear what happened to you. It just breaks her heart, especially because of all the efforts they're going to--"

"I want to see her tears," my mother interjects.

"She made all the right noises. She said she's open to talking to you. I guess it depends what kind of closure you want."

"Closure?" My mother cackles and walks away toward the kitchen. "They would just deny they did anything wrong."

I follow closely behind like an alley stalker. "Mom, they don't need to deny anything. They don't have any records or knowledge of the case. She won't even challenge you. You could tell them Bill Restivo showed up to the office Christmas party with a confederate flag as a pocket square and she wouldn't confirm or deny it. She'd say if something like that happened, they're extremely sorry. But you'd be filling in all the gaps yourself."

I backtrack and explain to her again how the Commission's case against Bell fell apart. By this point, I might even understand the technicalities of the case better than her. When I'm finished, she shakes her head.

"Between all of them, they screwed me up good and proper. By the end, I didn't know if my head was facing *left, right, or centre*."

"So," I continue, "I don't know if there's something specific you want to extract from Jennifer, or just tease her a little, but she's open to talking. It's *uncomfortable conversations that lead to action*."

"Action? Bell spent all that money and won."

"Then what is it that you want from her?"

"I feel like I haven't had justice. That's all."

"What would justice look like?"

"All the things I was denied as a worker. Restitution for the hurt and the insult. At the time, it was worth a million dollars."

"You want to ask her for a *million dollars*? I don't think she has that much authority. Her job description is to be sorry to hear about your experience. Department of strategic regret."

"You're laughing!" my mother exclaims, penetrating my deadpan. "Well, I can give her the documents. Maybe she can come down here and spend a few weeks in the basement going through--"

"No, mom, she won't do that either. She doesn't want to read the documents. Her job is to make you go away."

"Why do I want to go away? You *are* being funny. So, I'm supposed to provide her with entertainment and some peace of mind?"

I shrug. "And remind her there's still work to be done even at a progressive place like Bell Canada. And it will warm your heart knowing the strides Bell has made promoting diversity in their modern workplace."

"What makes you think I can help others when I can't help myself?" argues my mother, raising her voice. "Why would I want to go through the agony and the angst again?"

"She can acknowledge your suffering and be a compassionate ear, like a therapist. Maybe she can give you a deal on long distance."

"I bet it will give her a thrill to apologize."

"It's what she was made for."

This makes my mother laugh. "You make it sound like she's full of shit."

"Could be." I can't decide if it's more condescending for someone to be believed unconditionally, or to be doubted all the way to the Federal Court of Appeals. "She's a lawyer, so she knows full well when someone has no leverage. The case can't be reopened."

"Uh huh."

"But it got me thinking. Is it helpful to beg for an apology on behalf of a corporation, from someone like Jennifer, who can't even corroborate your story? Does anybody still alive even have the moral authority to apologize to you?"

"It's frustrating," admits my mother. "Or maybe an apology would help get it out of my system. These days, everybody's getting into Black Lives Matter and everything."

"I guess empty symbolism is important."

"I wonder if every Black person out there has had a bad experience like mine."

"Could be."

# 71. A BITTER TASTE

"I had a sad day yesterday, you know," says my mother as she enters the kitchen. "I made a big batch of cookies. I spent all day slaving in the kitchen, and when they were done, they looked *beautiful*. But then when I tasted one of them, it had a bitter taste, like something had burned. I tried another bite, and it was the same thing."

"So, I thought, what *on earth* is going on here?" She opens a small tin on the counter, its lid decorated with brightly coloured gingerbread people. Inside, a neatly tied transparent bag is packed with perfectly round shortbread, artfully topped with red and green maraschino cherries. "And when I went back to the fridge to check the margarine, the tub had been expired for *six years*. Try one and tell me if you can taste the difference."

"I'd rather not," I say. "You already told me they were no good. Besides, that shouldn't be enough to ruin the whole day. God knows I've had my share of baking mishaps."

"That was only the first thing." She closes the tin and tucks it into the cupboard. "Because then, I got to thinking about the Bell case. I had been getting my hopes up again, thinking it could go further. I had been thinking of ways of calling Mary Eberts. And that's when it crossed my mind, am I just going to *kill myself out* trying to get justice? It's been so hard on me all being alone in this thing for years."

"And now you're telling me the Commission made some big *goof*, and that after eight years they wanted me to start all over from square one. Were they out of their mind? I have been to hell and back. By the end of yesterday, I was distraught. I thought I had the worst day of my life."

"Worse days are possible," I say. I picture civil unrest, fiery infernos, and earthquake rubble before I recognize that my mother wants empathy rather than perspective. But she ignores me and retrieves her Catholic missal from the countertop.

"Then, I came across today's church reading, from

Ecclesiastes." She's bookmarked a page near the back and reads it aloud.

> But after a while, you must let go of what lies behind and press forward. If you don't, the past will destroy your future. Like the children of Israel, God wants you to let go of the past and take new ground. Don't spend the rest of your life mourning something you have lost. Go forward and don't look back.

"I thought, how strange to get this reading, today of all days. After finding out that those records are *gone*, like they never existed."

I want to say I've been changed, by learning that the gullet of history has swallowed all trace and memory of what once seemed an epic battle between good and evil. Changed by how time and the universe negate even the most pivotal trials of a lifetime. Changed by how they negate even the real Viola, now more a symbol than she ever was a person. She's forever diminished to *that theatre woman*. That ten-dollar bill is her dying gasp against the ravages of time. Was she ever much of a hairstylist?

"Bell and the Commission kept your employment records a little longer than you kept that margarine," I say instead. "Case or no case, somewhere there are two parallel universes where you're seventy-seven years old. In both of them, you've got an adult son. You're living comfortably in the suburbs. In both, there's a story about Bell, and the story just ends different. Who knows, maybe in one of them, you end up on the five-dollar bill."

My mother cackles. This seems to cheer her up.

## 72. FEATURING THAT LADY

"When I told the priest, he said we should make a movie out of it. I wanted *that lady* to play me. That Black actress."

"Halle Berry?"

"Not Halle Berry. The one who won an Academy Award for her first movie."

"Angela Bassett," I suggest, before unleashing a rapid-fire battery of names: "Erykah Badu. Oprah Winfrey.

Meryl Streep. Meryl Streep in blackface. Justin Trudeau in blackface. I mean, he was a drama teacher and everything."

"*Lupita Nyong'o*," my mother says triumphantly. "She's not a bad looking girl. Her hair is in the African style. I think she would do an amazing job. But you don't hear anything about her anymore."

"We're mid-pandemic," I say. "You don't hear much about anybody in Hollywood anymore."

"But you know what? I've been thinking that the Black people who are protesting in the United States had a better deal for their lives than I did. Because I was alone and Black, with no one to fight alongside me. There were only two of us in Prince Edward Island. And when I came out into the big city, they did nothing but take advantage of me."

"Mmmhmm."

"Here was somebody, top of my class in university, who graduated *cum laude*. Came to Toronto and got those extra qualifications in human resources, and they *would not* move me from that entry level position working beside people with a high school education. And because I was naïve and alone, they got away with it. And when I tried to stand up for myself, they made an ass out of me."

I nod, after a quick calculation that anything I say here will be inadequate.

"Never absent, never late for work. The way they used me hurts badly."

"Maybe Jennifer is right in a way," I suggest gently. "The world has made some progress since those days."

I'm not sure how she will react to this.

"Yes. Things are better now."

## 73. GRAFFITI ALLEY

Panic.

That's because I wake up in a void, a dream, unsure if it's night or day. When my phone vibrates, it takes me a moment to realize I've already answered it, that it's Jessica on the other end of the line. It's strange for *anyone* to call rather than text these days, but especially her. I fear the worst, a monsoon flood of adrenaline whose intensity surprises me. People who still make unannounced phone calls fall into two basic camps: my mother, and those bearing terrible news.

"You need to come down here *right now*," is all Jessica will say. The tremble in her voice suggests she's somewhere on the verge of laughing or crying.

"Why?" I stammer, then pause. I might well have added: "and where?"

"Come on, you know exactly where."

That's true. I feel foolish for even asking, and find myself bundled in my parka, tuque, and gloves before I'm aware of what's happening. How strange. I dash through the revolving doors of my apartment building, sprint upstream through the unnatural and ghostly emptiness of Yonge Street, festinating faster and faster until I'm in danger of toppling forward onto my face, managing to slow down only when I reach the familiar intersection with the hipster village of Queen Street West.

But here, the streets are suddenly transformed, impossibly crowded, and I find myself elbowing my way through a sea of writhing bodies. The faceless protesters push and jostle me forward in a manner both infuriating and impossible to resist. Around me, I hear the excruciating sounds of whistles, chanting, and a screaming loudspeaker.

Suffocating. The musk of warm bodies, of sweat, of moist wool. I'm lost, and the street signs are obstructed in all directions by insistent marchers and signs bearing illegible slogans. I can't be certain whether I, myself, am moving, or whether this implacable current is sweeping me forward. I can't see the colour of the sky. I can't recall if I brought my backpack when I left home, or whether it's been stripped from me in the tumult, but I'm certain I don't need it. I need nothing but my two hands.

Frantic. Because Jessica is waiting, but I don't understand how to get where I should be. In my rush, I forgot my phone. How could that be possible? How could this pulsating crowd be all that presently exists, whisking me down the avenue like a raft in an Amazon deluge? Panic.

Suddenly, it's Abagbe Adebayo. *Of course*, Abagbe would be here, precisely here. She's a much better standard-bearer for this Black collective than me, so she would have to be here. Glasses, nappy hair, big smile. I'm ashamed of myself.

But she, on the other hand, smiles warmly. "Didn't think I'd ever see you here. I wasn't even sure if you self-identify as Black, but it doesn't really matter. Your mother would be happy."

I grin foolishly. I try to respond but find myself a tongue-tied buffoon with nothing profound to add.

"Don't worry," she says, her face radiating benevolence. "I don't make assumptions. Or I try not to, anyway."

With that, she's gone. I look around for her nappy hair and her Cheshire grin, but there's no trace. Disoriented, I dance around the corner into the chaotic maze between storefronts and low buildings, where the turnover of dozens of street murals has been almost universal. Graffiti alley.

I don't know how I've surfaced here, but it is nothing short of miraculous. My relief buckles my knees. The crowd has vanished like morning fog. Where there were once colourful caricatures of schools of fishes, pop culture icons, and counterculural art, the alley is now almost entirely adorned with political and revolutionary images – the black and white ghost of Malcolm X standing sentry in one doorway, the faces of young Black men and women gunned down by American police officers resurrected on the brick walls, a spray-painted banner reading *Black Lives Matter* that neatly covers the length of an entire building. It's a bright, cold day, and filthy snow lines the edges of the alley.

I find Jessica standing there, waiting, bundled in a bright blue parka that gives her the appearance of Paddington Bear. Her cheeks are a shade of pink that betrays having been outside far too long.

"Did you crawl here on your hands and knees? It's fucking *cold*."

I don't answer. She gestures upward with her chin, and my eyes instinctively follow.

"Oh my God," I say. "You have to be kidding me."

"Insane, right? I knew a guy who does this stuff, and he thought it was sweet what you were doing with your mom's story. To be honest, I didn't believe he would actually do it."

I smile, too stunned to know how to react. The mural is easily the largest in the alley. It has been lovingly painted by hand, like the *Creation of Adam* crowning the Sistine Chapel. Head to torso, it measures at least twelve feet high and perhaps another forty in width. Its blue shades are muted, lending it an imposing and dignified appearance.

It is a Canadian five-dollar bill, my mother's face where Sir Wilfred Laurier's should rightfully be. Beside us, a young white couple is posing for a selfie beneath the mural, looking for the ideal angle with which to capture its enormity, and I don't know why I hadn't noticed them before.

They catch my eye, and they smile politely. When their gaze lingers too long, I smile back and then blurt out after some hesitation: "That's my mom, you know?"

"Actually?" The girl looks up at her partner and her polite smile erupts into an unguarded grin, teeth brilliant and blinding. "That's amazing!" she exclaims, unable to contain her emotion. "I could never understand why Viola Desmond was such a big deal. A *theatre*! She didn't go through half what your mother did."

"I think you're right," I hear myself say. Then, without warning, they've disappeared deeper into the shadows of the alley.

Jessica and I remain in place. I gaze up at the enormous portrait. After a few minutes, we continue our walk through the graffiti alley, and I have the feeling of walking in sunlight.

"Don't you think all this is a little…I don't know. Over the top?"

Jessica stops to think.

"You complained Viola Desmond wasn't a hero. And now, after all this, you can't accept your own mother as a hero. Maybe you just like to complain."

"I don't know. That's not it. Sometimes, I just think everyone has run into some adversity in their lives. I mean, has anyone's life ever been one unbroken, glorious journey from success to success?"

"Who are you trying to convince?" asks Jessica. "Me, or yourself?"

Two tears trickle from the sides of my nose. It was all right, everything was all right, the struggle was finished. I had won the victory over myself.

And then I wake up.

Manufactured by Amazon.ca
Bolton, ON